STD ~~block~~ 945.083

8.99

The Italian Risorgimento

HISTORICAL CONNECTIONS

Series editors
Geoffrey Crossick, University of Essex
John Davis, University of Connecticut
Joanna Innes, Somerville College, University of Oxford
Tom Scott, University of Liverpool

Already published

The Decline of Industrial Britain 1870–1980
Michael Dintenfass

The French Revolution
Gwynne Lewis

The Rise of Regional Europe
Christopher Harvie

The Remaking of the British Working Class
Michael Savage and Andrew Miles

Forthcoming titles

Catholic Politics in Europe 1918–1945
Martin Conway

The Unification of Germany
Michael John

*Population Policies in Twentieth-Century Dictatorships
and Democracies*
Maria Quine

Nationalism in the USSR
Stephen Jones

Fascism in Italy and Germany
Alex de Grand

Popular Politics in Nineteenth-Century England
Rohan McWilliam

Environment and History
William Beinart and Peter Coates

The Italian Risorgimento

State, society and national unification

Lucy Riall

London and New York

First published 1994
by Routledge
11 New Fetter Lane, London EC4P 4EE

Simultaneously published in the USA and Canada
by Routledge
29 West 35th Street, New York, NY 10001

© 1994 Lucy Riall

Typeset in Times by
Ponting–Green Publishing Services, Chesham, Bucks

Printed and bound in Great Britain by
Clays Ltd, St Ives plc

Printed on acid free paper

British Library Cataloguing in Publication Data
A catalogue record for this book is available from the
British Library.

Library of Congress Cataloging in Publication Data
Riall, Lucy
    The Italian Risorgimento: state, society, and national
unification / Lucy Riall.
        p.   cm. – (Historical connections)
    Includes bibliographical references and index.
    1. Italy–History–1849–1870.
    2. Italy–History–1849–1870–Historiography.
    I. Title.   II. Series.
    DG552.R46   1994
    945'.08–dc20   93–33882

ISBN 0–415–05775–2

For MCM

Contents

Series editors' preface

Historical Connections is a new series of short books on important historical topics and debates, written primarily for those studying and teaching history. The books will offer original and challenging works of synthesis that will make new themes accessible, or old themes accessible in new ways, build bridges between different chronological periods and different historical debates, and encourage comparative discussion in history.

If the study of history is to remain exciting and creative, then the tendency to fragmentation must be resisted. The inflexibility of older assumptions about the relationship between economic, social, cultural and political history has been exposed by recent historical writing, but the impression has sometimes been left that history is little more than a chapter of accidents. This series will insist on the importance of processes of historical change, and it will explore the connections within history: connections between different layers and forms of historical experience, as well as connections that resist the fragmentary consequences of new forms of specialism in historical research.

Historical Connections will put the search for these connections back at the top of the agenda by exploring new ways of uniting the different strands of historical experience, and by affirming the importance of studying change and movement in history.

Geoffrey Crossick
John Davies
Joanna Innes
Tom Scott

Acknowledgements

I wish to thank John Davis, who invited me to write this book and gave up so much of his time to help me with it. If readers of the book find it helpful, much of the credit for this must go to him. I am also very grateful to Geoffrey Crossick, David Lavan, Silvana Patriarca, Michael Sugrue and Mike Broers who read earlier versions of the book and who all offered useful comments, criticisms and suggestions. Further thanks are due to Paul Ginsborg, John Dickie and Pamela Sharpe for their advice on crucial points, and to Eliza Kentridge for preparing the maps. Of course, none of these people is responsible for what follows. The University of Essex gave me study leave in order to write the book, and the History Department at Johns Hopkins University provided me with a stimulating environment and excellent facilities in which to complete it.

I would also like to thank Jon Thorn, Mark McDonald, Sarah Gavaghan, my parents and, above all, Mark McGaw for their company and intellectual stimulation during the times when I wasn't writing the book.

Chronology

1796–9 France invades and occupies the Italian mainland.

1814–15 Congress of Vienna partially restores pre-Napoleonic rulers and boundaries. Austria is established as the dominant power in Restoration Italy: Lombardy-Venetia become provinces of the Austrian Empire and protective alliances are signed with the Papal States and the Two Sicilies.

1820–1 Constitutional revolutions in the Two Sicilies and in Piedmont briefly challenge Restoration government, but are suppressed with the aid of the Austrian army.

1830–1 Revolutionary uprisings in Central Italy are suppressed by Austrian and French intervention.

1831 Giuseppe Mazzini organises 'Young Italy' to fight for 'the conquest of Independence, Unity, Liberty for Italy'.
Carlo Alberto becomes king of Piedmont.
The European Powers sign a Memorandum calling for reform in the Papal States.

1834–7 A series of Mazzinian uprisings and expeditions take place throughout Italy. The repression of 'Young Italy' and its infiltration by police spies forces Mazzini into exile in London.

1843 The publication of Vincenzo Gioberti's *Del primato morale e civile degli italiani* marks the emergence of the idea of an Italian confederation under the Pope ('Neo-Guelphism') and of moderate liberalism as a political movement.

1846   Election of Pio IX as Pope. A number of reforms are introduced in the Papal States.

1847   The periodical *Il Risorgimento* begins publication in Turin under the editorship of Camillo Benso di Cavour.

1848   A revolution in Palermo in January is followed by a series of revolutions and disturbances throughout Italy, which lead to the granting of constitutions limiting monarchical power.
In March, after a revolution in Vienna and the flight of Metternich, revolutions take place in Venice and Milan (where the Austrian army is driven out of the city during the celebrated *cinque giornate* or 'five days'). A Republic is declared in Venice. Piedmont declares war on Austria but is defeated at the battle of Custoza in July and signs an armistice. In May, Ferdinando II carries out a coup to restore monarchical power in Naples.

1849   In January, the Pope flees Rome and a Republic is declared. Mazzini invites delegates from all over Italy to a Constituent Assembly to discuss Italian unification. Grand Duke Leopoldo flees Tuscany and a republican government is established in Florence.
Piedmont again declares war on Austria and is again defeated at the battle of Novara in March. Carlo Alberto abdicates and his son Vittorio Emanuele II becomes king of Piedmont.
In April, Bourbon power is re-established in Sicily. A French army intervenes against the Roman Republic to restore the Pope.
Under Giuseppe Garibaldi's leadership, the Roman Republic holds out until July, when it is finally defeated and the Pope is restored. Grand Duke Leopoldo returns to Florence.
The besieged Venetian Republic falls to the Austrians in August.

1852   Cavour becomes prime minister of Piedmont and introduces a programme of economic and political reform.

1853   A Mazzinian, anti-Austrian insurrection in Milan is easily suppressed.

1854–6 Piedmont participates in the Crimean War. At the Congress of Paris, the 'Italian Question' is raised.

1857   The ill-fated expedition to Sapri in Southern Italy led by Carlo Pisacane causes a crisis in Mazzinian circles.

The Italian National Society is established by former Mazzinians to agitate for Italian unification under Piedmontese leadership.

1858   In January, an attempt is made on Napoleon III's life by an ex-Mazzinian (Felice Orsini).

In July, a secret pact is signed between Napoleon III and Cavour, whereby France offers military assistance to Piedmont, who will provoke a war with Austria; Piedmont will receive Lombardy and Venetia; France will receive Nice and Savoy (previously ruled by Piedmont).

1859   Austria declares war on Piedmont in April, and France comes to Piedmont's assistance.

After the battles of Magenta and Solferino, Napoleon III signs an armistice with Austria at Villafranca. Piedmont receives Lombardy but not Venetia. In a fury, Cavour resigns as prime minister.

1860   In January, Cavour returns to power in Piedmont. In March, plebiscites in Central Italy lead to the union of Tuscany and Emilia (comprising the Duchies of Parma and Modena and the Papal Legations) with Piedmont-Lombardy. In return for French agreement to the union, Nice and Savoy are ceded to France.

In April, Garibaldi leads the expedition of the 'Thousand' to Sicily. Between May and July he conquers the whole of the Two Sicilies, and prepares to march on Rome.

The Piedmontese army invades the Papal States in September in order to forestall Garibaldi's advance on Rome. Garibaldi hands over Southern Italy to Piedmont.

In October, plebiscites in Southern Italy vote for union with Piedmont.

1861   A Kingdom of Italy is declared in March, with Turin as its capital; Vittorio Emanuele II of Piedmont becomes Vittorio Emanuele II of Italy.

1862   Garibaldi's attempt to march on Rome is halted by Italian troops at Aspromonte.

1864   The 'convention of September' moves the Italian capital from Turin to Florence.

1866   Italy participates in the Austro-Prussian war on the Prussian side. After Austria's defeat by Prussia (and despite Italy's defeat by Austria), Venetia is ceded to Italy.

1867   A further attempt by Garibaldi to march on Rome is halted by Papal troops at Mentana.

1870   French troops are withdrawn from Rome to fight in the Franco-Prussian war. Rome is occupied by Italian troops, and is declared the capital of Italy. The Pope refuses to recognise the legitimacy of the new state, and declares himself a 'prisoner of the Vatican'.

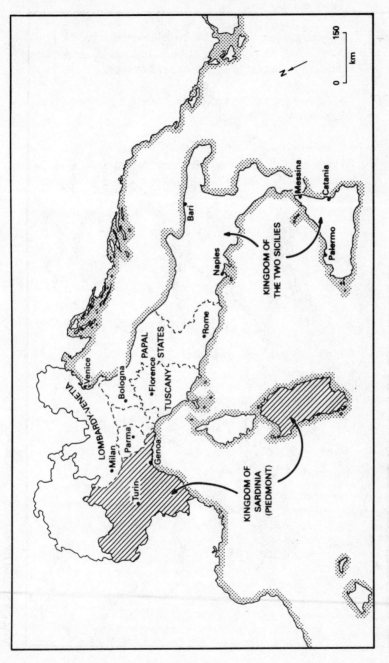

Map 1 Italy's Restoration states 1815

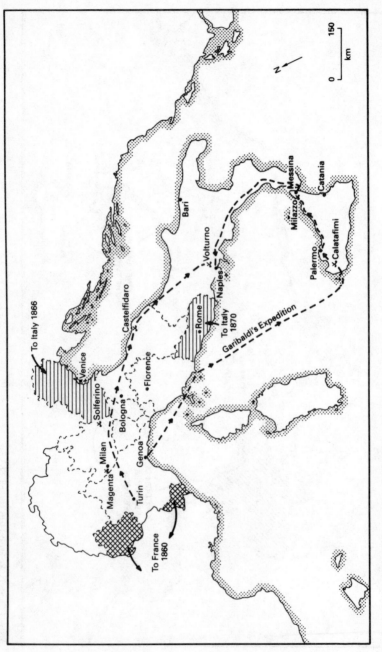

Map 2 Italy and the events of 1859–1860

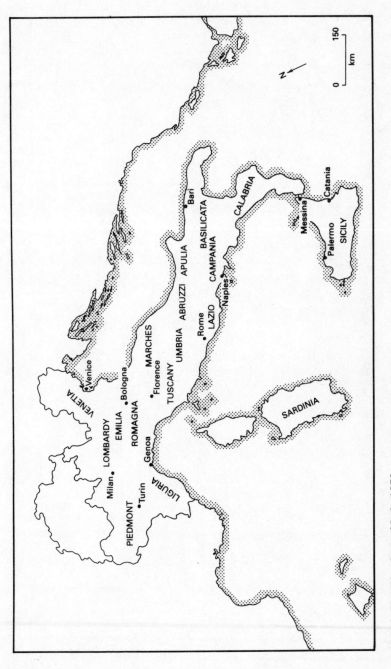

Map 3 The Kingdom of Italy 1870

1 The Risorgimento and Italian history

In Italian history, as in Italian politics, the Risorgimento has played a central role. Like the experience of the French Revolution or German unification, the Risorgimento is considered to be a defining moment in Italy's history, the period when Italy becomes a 'nation' and enters the 'modern' world. Through the Risorgimento, the modern Italian state acquires its 'founding fathers' (Cavour, Mazzini, Garibaldi) and its political ideals (liberalism, nationalism, republicanism). Conceptually, the Risorgimento has also been crucial to Italian historiography. It describes a number of different transformations – the collapse of the *ancien régime* and the development of a parliamentary system, the breakdown of traditional rural society and the birth of modern, urban life, the transition from a feudal to a capitalist economy and the replacement of local or regional identities by a single national culture – all of which have been central to present-day understanding of historical change. The political, social, economic and cultural experiences of Italians from 1815 to 1945 (and, arguably, beyond) are explained, interpreted and assessed on the basis of these 'modernising' processes.

The functional importance of the Risorgimento to both Italian politics and Italian historiography has made this short period (1815–60) one of the most contested and controversial in modern Italian history. Just as politicians have squabbled, from 1861 onwards, over the Risorgimento's political legacies, so have historians of the Risorgimento quarrelled about the primary determinants of change and modernisation. At the centre of these debates is a set of rhetorical devices first employed by Risorgimento liberals to denigrate the governments of Restoration Italy. The term 'Risorgimento', literally translated, means 'resurgence' and refers to a common, idealised past as well as to a less than perfect present. Mazzinian democrats were particularly successful in offering a series of heroic alternatives against which the everyday realities of Restoration Italy could be judged. They depicted Italians as the hapless victims of domestic and foreign oppression who could be liberated and empowered through a revolutionary war of 'national resurgence'. Ironically, after 1860, these images bequeathed a pervasive sense of failure to united Italy, and fuelled a bitter political struggle. Nostalgia for the often imagined glories of the Risorgimento characterised much political debate after 1860.[1] Historical analysis also concerned itself with Italy's inability to 'resurge' and with the 'peculiarities' of Italian historical development.

The experiences of fascism and world war also cast a retrospective shadow over the Risorgimento and divided its historians into mutually hostile camps. In an attempt to re-evaluate the mythology of national unification against the background of liberal Italy's collapse, two conflicting accounts of Italian unification emerged, one published by the idealist philosopher Benedetto Croce in 1928, the other written during the fascist period by the imprisoned Marxist activist Antonio Gramsci (but published only in 1949).[2] These two opposing currents of historical analysis share a common preoccupation with the apparent failure of Liberal Italy to live up to the aspirations and expectations of the Risorgimento.

Croce's primary aim in writing his history of Italy was, according to Federico Chabod, to defend the achievements of Italian liberalism.[3] The leaders of the Historic Right (or *Destra Storica*), the architects of Italian unification in 1860, were presented as men of a noble and self-sacrificing character, 'a spiritual aristocracy of upright and loyal gentlemen' in Croce's words.[4] Croce argued that Liberal Italy's short-comings could be attributed to decisions made by the *Destra Storica*'s successors, and equally to the enormous problems that all Italy's leaders faced. Despite these political, financial and diplomatic difficulties Italy's leaders had always maintained their commitment to the liberal parliamentary system until the First World War. Croce insisted that it was only the war that destroyed this political system and made the rise of fascism possible. As such, he denied any causal connection between Italian liberalism and Italian fascism. Fascism was a historical 'parenthesis', an aberration produced by the war. The political ideals of fascism, in particular its commitment to a one-party state, were the 'antithesis' of liberalism.

Although influenced by Croce's idealist philosophy, Gramsci totally opposed his political and historical arguments. Gramsci saw instead a series of links between fascism and liberalism, and he traced both experiences to the tensions generated by class struggle in the Risorgimento. He depicted the Risorgimento as a 'passive revolution', where the conservative ('moderate') liberals had out-manœuvered the revolutionary liberals (republican democrats) and come to a compromise with the existing 'feudal' order. But the price of this compromise was a permanent breach between the Italian state and Italian civil society, characterised by chronic political instability and endemic social disorder. Fascism, Gramsci argued, was the direct product of this situation. It was an attempt by a weak bourgeoisie to recast a collapsing political system, counter class unrest and, specifically, to defeat a socialist revolution.

The effect of Gramsci's dialogue with Croce was to set up a series of historical oppositions that dominated Risorgimento historiography in the post-1945 period. Underlying these oppositions was a fundamental, and highly politicised, conflict between idealism and historical materialism. The Crocean (or liberal) depiction of political harmony was challenged by the Gramscian (or Marxist) one of class conflict. Gramsci claimed that the chronology chosen by Croce (1871–1915) artificially excluded the moments of conflict to create a peaceful and progressive, but distorted, image of nineteenth-century Italy.[5] As such, an account that analysed national progress was countered by one that analysed structural backwardness, and a narrative that stressed glorious moments and heroic action met one that stressed internal divisions and political repression.

These oppositions, and the political context of post-war, cold-war Italy in which they were set, generated a great amount of historical debate and research. The dynamics of this debate are very evident in political histories of the Risorgimento. Dominating the Marxist approach is a relentless search for counterfactuals, a search for evidence of a viable democratic alternative to the 'passive revolution' led by moderate liberals. Marxist historians tend to emphasise the potential for revolutionary change in the Risorgimento and the differences between moderates and democrats. Franco della Peruta is, for example, critical of both moderate and democratic leaderships, but analyses in particular the reasons for the democrats' failure to establish a basis for mass action among the peasantry.[6]

Liberal historians, by contrast, stress the significant barriers to political and economic progress in Risorgimento Italy. Placing political action in the context of Italy's dependence on foreign powers, its internal disunity, its reactionary rulers and its economic backwardness, they argue that the scale of the liberal achievement was truly impressive. According to Rosario Romeo, Cavour's 'audacious' programme of reform without revolution was without parallel in Europe.[7] More generally, the economic dynamism and intellectual vigour of the moderate liberals is contrasted favourably to the insurrectionary and utopian 'fantasies' of Mazzinian democrats.

Debates about the economic and social aspects of the Risorgimento revolve around a similar set of oppositions. In the early 1950s, Gino Luzzato took issue with the Marxist identification of the Risorgimento with the bourgeoisie, arguing that the lack of industrial development before 1860 had seriously inhibited the development of this class.[8] Romeo maintained that it was utterly unrealistic to discuss the possibility of an agrarian revolution in Southern Italy, led by the bourgeoisie, during the Risorgimento; the Marxist preoccupation with this issue masked, he suggested, a more basic concern with the possibility of revolution in their own time. Had such a revolution been possible during the Risorgimento it would have inhibited the commercialisation of agriculture and retarded the industrialisation of Northern Italy.[9]

In this way, Marxist and liberal historians existed in a dialectical relationship of their own in which the ultimate success or failure of the Risorgimento and national unification was endlessly debated. In fact, Luzzato's narrow economic definition of the bourgeoisie and his conceptualisation of 'industrialisation' as the rapid growth and concentration of mechanised manufacturing industry implicitly accepts the same rigid economic categories as Marxists. Similarly, by arguing that a peasant revolution would have been detrimental to the subsequent development of Italian industry, Romeo adopts the same teleological view of the Risorgimento (as leading inexorably to industrialisation, or to Southern 'backwardness') that he criticises in the Marxist account.

The Marxist and the liberal approaches to the Risorgimento share a common need to explain the significance of the moderate liberal victory in 1860 in terms of the subsequent disappointments of liberal Italy. In both accounts, modern Italy's 'deviation' from a more general bourgeois-democratic (and European) norm is assumed and explained. Within this national/liberal framework certain political and social realities are privileged over others. Most historians of Italy simply assumed that the Restoration governments of 1815 to 1860 were reactionary and, therefore, of little significance.[10] As such, few historians looked at the policies pursued by Papal governors, Austrian administrators or Bourbon kings in much detail. Relations between and among social classes were also assessed as a struggle between 'progressive' and 'reactionary' forces, where the progressive was identified with a liberal ideology or an urban, commercial bourgeoisie. In this light, the source of modern Italy's 'deviation' was easy to identify: it was caused by the survival of feudal 'remnants' into the modern world and by the failure (whether political, ideological or economic) to resolve political and class conflict in Italy in favour of progress and modernity.

Although the contributions of British and American historians to Risorgimento historiography since 1945 have been less overtly polemical than those of their Italian counterparts, they too reflect this conceptual distinction between progress and reaction. They have also tended strongly to reflect changing Anglo-Saxon attitudes towards Italy. The most famous British Italianist, Denis Mack Smith, created a furore in Italy with a series of works published during the 1950s which appeared to criticise leading Risorgimento figures and disparage Liberal Italy's achievements.[11] In his first book, a reconstruction of the events of 1860 ('the *annus mirabilis* of the Risorgimento' in his words),[12] Mack Smith depicted Cavour as a wily, inconsistent politician and the achievement of unification as a series of mistakes and expediencies. Only Garibaldi, emerging from Mack Smith's narrative as a realistic but committed popular leader, survived with his honour intact. Thus, without being influenced by Gramsci, Mack Smith placed himself firmly in the Risorgimento-as-failure camp.[13]

This view of the Risorgimento was endorsed by most British and American historians. Their tendency to analyse Italian unity from the standpoint of what came after is particularly evident in a collection of essays published in 1970 and entitled *Italy from Risorgimento to Fascism. An Inquiry into the Origins of the Totalitarian State*, but it is implicit in much other work on this period.[14] What seems to lie behind this type of analysis is profound disillusionment at the failure of Italian governments either to embody the ideals of the Risorgimento or to fulfil the aspirations of its people. As such, the attempts by Mack Smith and others to demystify the 'legends' of Risorgimento historiography have to be seen in the context of the changing fortunes of Italian liberalism. British enthusiasm for Italian unity, perhaps most strikingly expressed by George Macaulay Trevelyan in his *Garibaldi* trilogy, started to decline as early as World War One.[15] By 1945, with the experience of fascism and World War Two overshadowing Italy's image abroad, this enthusiasm had changed to disappointment and condescension.

A combination of disappointed expectations and deep political divisions produced a set of historiographical parameters for interpreting the Risorgimento, identifying economic 'backwardness', a 'distorted' social transformation and political corruption/timidity as the causes of liberal failure. During the 1980s, however, these parameters began to change. In part, as Paolo Macry points out, this change was generational: many of the protagonists in post-war debates reached retirement age during the 1980s.[16] A younger generation of historians, born after 1945, started to question many of the basic assumptions of Risorgimento historiography. Furthermore, in a broader cultural and political sense, the nineteenth-century faith in economic progress and individual liberty has increasingly seemed, during the last decade, to have little relevance for current political problems. For Paolo Macry, the personal links of empathy and memory, which tied historians of the previous generation to the 'century of their fathers', have now disappeared.[17]

The teleology of both the Marxist and the liberal approaches to the Risorgimento has come in for particular criticism from 'revisionist' historians. The idea of modernisation, implicit in the Marxist concept of 'dual' (political and economic) revolution as well as in the idealist concept of progress, is now treated with suspicion. An increasing reliance on alternative historical models and methodologies also reflects the Risorgimento's declining 'hegemony' over Italian politics and intellectual life.[18] One historian, Franco Rizzi, has complained of the Risorgimento's holding the nineteenth century 'hostage', dominating the historical agenda and blocking other avenues of enquiry.[19]

An effect of these changes has been a switch of focus to other stages of Italy's 'modernising' process, perhaps most notably to the period of rapid industrialisation in the late nineteenth century. Histories of nineteenth-century Italy also now focus more on social change, the history of family and gender and, to a lesser extent, cultural change, than they do on Risorgimento politics. The influence of other disciplines, perhaps most notably anthropology, is very clear. In addition, and in contrast to the liberal/Marxist debate which always emphasised the national specificities of Italy's path to modernity, this 'revisionist' historiography adopts an explicitly comparative perspective which focuses on regions and localities rather than nations. Historical research in Italy has thus come to involve a new plurality where the nation state is no longer the privileged unit of comparison, and the importance of the Risorgimento is no longer taken for granted. National unification then acquires a different significance as a partial solution to specific problems, rather than as a decisive break (however flawed in practice) with a feudal past.

This change of direction has meant that many of the causal connections at the heart of nineteenth-century historiography are being questioned. Some local studies have been particularly innovative, linking analyses of family structure to economic developments and in turn back to political activity. In a study of the formation of an agrarian middle class in the Po valley, Alberto Banti argues that the apparently feudal reliance on land ownership and kinship structure masks the

dynamic action of a rational, self-interested bourgeoisie.[20] The implications of this kind of work are far-reaching. Taken as a whole, they
undermine any simple identification of the bourgeoisie with urbanisation, industrialisation or, indeed, liberal politics. In addition, they
give force to analyses of Italy's economic development that emphasise
the potential for growth and adaptation in the countryside. Not surprisingly, therefore, the more traditional interpretations of Italy's
'Southern Question' have also been challenged. A number of historians,
most notably Piero Bevilacqua, have begun to question the images of
backwardness, economic immobilism and political corruption long
associated with the South. They suggest that these images, invoking as
they do a sense of 'otherness', involve unrealistic comparisons with
Northern Italy and with Europe as a whole.[21]

The revisionist historiography of nineteenth-century Italy thus challenges the periodisation, methodologies and interpretations of previous
historiographies. In particular, revisionist historiography rejects the use
of categories such as 'class' and 'nation'. As such, it reflects and can
contribute to similar historiographical debates taking place in France,
Germany and the Anglo-Saxon world. Marxist analyses of German
liberalism have come under attack for their reliance on models of
political and economic development that are artificially constructed
from the English and French experiences.[22] Recent research has indi-
cated that the political and economic 'success' against which Italy (and,
in a different way, Germany) is compared so unfavourably tends to
evaporate with closer analysis or when different questions are asked.[23]

The revision in French revolutionary and British liberal history
implies that no single path to liberal bourgeois democracy exists.
Moreover, Arno Mayer has argued that historians' preoccupations with
the revolutionary changes of the nineteenth century have clouded their
perceptions of underlying continuities and the ways in which the *ancien
régime* survived into the twentieth century. The capacity of pre-industrial
elites to adapt successfully to the advent of capitalism seems not to be
exceptional at all, but a feature of all European societies in this period.[24]
It can thus be argued that Italy's 'deviation' has been invented by its
historians, influenced by deterministic models of political and economic
development as well as by the drastic experiences of fascism and war.

Where does the disintegration of these long-established categories
leave the historian of Risorgimento politics? One possibility is to focus
more specifically on the governments of Restoration Italy. Partly as a
reaction to nationalist historiography, a tendency to stress the positive
aspects of Restoration government and the extent of local variation has
developed. The most obvious beneficiary of this historiographical trend

is the Austrian administration of Lombardy and Venetia, the Risorgimento symbol of reactionary and oppressive misgovernment. New research, led most notably by Marco Meriggi, points to the relative responsiveness of the centre to local demands and the role played by government in overseeing rapid economic growth in this region.[25] Narcisso Nada also stresses the role played by King Carlo Alberto of Piedmont (1831–1849) in bringing about political and economic reform, and thus his responsibility for the liberal transformation that followed in the 1850s.[26]

One result of this research has been to place the crisis of Restoration government and the unification of Italy in a broader European context. Italian unification is seen, not as the inevitable result of national liberal 'resurgence' or the rise of a new class, but as the outcome of different, sometimes contradictory, processes. These processes can be loosely identified as the formation of modern states, the growth of a national culture based on language and literacy and the development of a capitalist economy.[27] They evolved, in Italy as elsewhere, over a long time-period and provide a strong element of continuity between the eighteenth century, the Risorgimento and after. State formation, in particular, is conceived as a process independent of changes in the social and economic structure and driven by forces (the political and bureaucratic elites) inside the state itself. This conceptualisation of state formation as an autonomous process owes more to Weber than to Marx, and further challenges the hitherto established equation of industrial capitalism with the rise of parliamentary democracy.

One problem, however, with the recent literature on state formation in Italy is that, unlike in Germany, no detailed critique of Marxist historiography has emerged.[28] The absence of such a critique has led, according to John Davis, to a conceptual confusion where Weberian categories mingle with Marxist or idealist ones.[29] Moreover, this new approach to state formation itself privileges certain types of state/society relationships, specifically the one between central government and local elites. Despite a new emphasis on the conditions of the rural and urban poor, the significance of class conflict is undermined and the role played by mass action in Italian unification becomes subordinated to the one played by elites. The attitude of the Church towards the process of state formation and towards Italian nationalism is almost entirely ignored.

The absence of the Church in revisionist accounts is very revealing. The Church played a central role in the Risorgimento; its opposition to nationalism and national unification accounts for many of the weaknesses of the nationalist movement. In their neglect of the Church, revisionists are part of a secular tradition in Italian life that dates back to the Risorgimento itself and links revisionists to both liberal and Marxist historians. A further feature of revisionist historiography – its almost exclusive reliance on structural explanation – also seems to owe much to the influence of Marxist historians. The revisionist emphasis on state, economy and culture (here understood primarily in a structural sense) involves a neglect of the role played by ideology in national unification. Little attention is paid to political discourse and political struggle and, for the most part, the literature on Risorgimento politics remains unaltered from a decade ago.

Perhaps more surprisingly, a tendency to endorse earlier liberal assessments of Risorgimento politics can also be found in some revisionist work. Raffaele Romanelli, for example, stresses the great liberal project of the Historic Right and the obstacles that they faced.[30] The impracticability of a revolutionary option is implicitly suggested by such an account, as well as by analyses that emphasise the 'good sense' of Restoration rulers.

The Risorgimento may well be an outmoded historical concept. Nevertheless, some belief or claim to embody a 'resurgent' Italy motivated Italian liberals and was used to demoralise Restoration rulers. During the last decade, an important reassessment of nineteenth-century Italian art, long overshadowed by the early-modern period, has also taken place. Interestingly, however, the tendency in this field has been to emphasise rather than underplay the significance of the Risorgimento.[31] Nationalist aspirations, and the struggle between Italian liberals to promote or appropriate them, affected the process of structural change in nineteenth-century Italy. Moreover, the great strength of Gramsci's account – and in this it has not yet been fully challenged or superseded – was that by focusing on the tensions between class and ideology and between leadership and social structure, it forced historians to look at national unification in terms of a broader struggle for power.

The new historiography, while challenging categories such as class and nation, has not developed an alternative means of conceptualising political action. Reflecting on the Austrian administration of Venetia, David Lavan has written that too many Risorgimento historians have been inclined to over-emphasise moments of crisis and conflict; as a result, periods of peaceful change are overshadowed and the experiences of Restoration government are seen as little more than preludes to insurrection.[32] However, the same mistake in reverse, which Gramsci warned against, should also be avoided. The reality of conflict and crisis in nineteenth-century Italy tends, in revisionist historiography, to be neglected. Nationalism is ignored rather than explained. Current analyses rightly reject the rigid categories of 'dual revolution' but they fail to provide an answer to what remains, for better or worse, a fundamental question: why did national unification happen at all?

This book is intended in part as a guide to the different ways in which the Risorgimento and Italian unification has been, and is being, interpreted. As such, it takes a broadly thematic rather than a narrative approach. An outline chronology and maps are provided as an indicator of the main events and geography of the Risorgimento. To help orient the reader, a brief summary of events is also given at the beginning of the next chapter. Those seeking a more detailed narrative account should consult the general surveys written by Stuart Woolf, Derek Beales, Harry Hearder and Frank Coppa.[33] The bibliographical section at the end of the book offers suggestions for more in-depth study.

In the chapters that follow, I look at Restoration government, economy and society – issues identified by Risorgimento liberals as obstacles to progress and change in Italy. Chapter 2 considers the attempts of Restoration rulers to establish stable regimes in the Italian peninsula between 1815 and 1860; Chapters 3 and 4 analyse society and economy in Restoration Italy. Chapter 5 discusses the character and impact of Italian nationalism. My aim in these chapters is, first, to provide a basis for understanding Italian unification. My second aim is to re-examine critically the attitudes of historians to the Risorgimento and Italian unification. Is it viable to see the Restoration states as reactionary survivors of the *ancien régime*, and can Italian historians analyse the economy and society in terms of a tension between progress and backwardness? Should national unification be explained either as a failed revolution or as the culmination of the Risorgimento, however it is defined? If not, how else can national unification be explained? The concluding chapter, Chapter 6, reassesses the concept of 'Risorgimento' in the light of historical revisionism.

2 The Risorgimento and Restoration government

INTRODUCTION: THE CRISIS OF THE OLD ORDER, THE VIENNA SETTLEMENT AND THE RISORGIMENTO

The origins of Italy's Risorgimento are usually placed in the pan-European crisis of the 'old order' which took place at the end of the eighteenth century. Within the city and regional states of the Italian peninsula, this crisis was associated with conflicts over reform. In particular, the efforts made by Italian rulers to build up more centralised and efficient bureaucracies ran into financial and political difficulties. Attempts to raise revenue through increased taxation were also unpopular and often unsuccessful, while both the Church and the nobility resented the attack on their special privileges and their position in the political hierarchy.

Institutional reform proved disruptive, whether relatively successful (as in Lombardy or Tuscany) or unsuccessful (as in Southern Italy or the Papal States). Growing economic and social problems added to the scale of the crisis facing the Italian states. These problems were caused in part by government efforts to commercialise agriculture through the abolition of feudal entails (part of the general effort to undermine noble and religious privilege) and the creation of an agrarian middle class. The rural poor, marginalised by economic developments as well as by the attack on the Church, suffered most from these reforms. Rapid population growth increased their problems still further. Popular upheaval from below, often encouraged by the feudal nobility and the Church, became at this time a feature of the Italian countryside.

The French invasions and occupations of the 1790s and 1800s also set the scene for the Risorgimento. Bitter counter-revolutionary violence, often reflecting the social and political divisions of the pre-revolutionary era, characterised the French period in Northern and Southern Italy. In addition, however, French rule brought many innovations. Particularly during the Napoleonic period, the Italian economies became more closely tied to the French economy, a process that damaged many domestic industries but that also helped to bring about infrastructural improvements. The attack on the Church's economic and political power was intensified.

Recent histories of French rule in Italy have emphasised the impact of political, administrative and judicial reforms and the continuities between the Napoleonic era and the Restoration. These reforms are seen to be decisive in the formation of modern states in many parts of Italy. As a result, the establishment of constitutions, the codification of laws and the modernisation of bureaucracies during the French period take on a greater significance than before. Alfonso Scirocco argues, for example, that the introduction of a new administrative system in the Kingdom of Naples permanently altered the way in which relations between the state and civil society were structured and understood. On the one hand, administrative centralisation was resented and resisted by local power-holders while, on the other, the new bureaucratic arrangements created employment opportunities for new elites.[1]

As such, and throughout Italy, French rule created new sources of social mobility and political tension. Administrative centralisation continued to be a controversial issue long after the end of French rule. The 'new men' who entered the administrations during the Napoleonic period got a taste of the political influence that had hitherto been confined to a more closed elite. They were very reluctant to relinquish their power after Napoleon's defeat. The experiences of the French occupations also suggested that political and economic change could lead to popular upheaval and counter-revolutionary violence. As a recent study has pointed out, recurring fears of the popular counter-revolution experienced in the French period constrained the actions of liberals and radicals in the Risorgimento.[2]

As well as being a harbinger of future tensions, the French occupation dealt a severe blow to the structures of *ancien régime* governments. The disruptions of foreign occupation, together with frequent alterations of territorial frontiers, undermined their legitimacy. The growth of organised political opposition during the revolutionary and Napoleonic periods was a powerful indicator of subsequent political developments. After 1814, movements of opposition began to appeal to nationalism and liberalism against the Restoration states. The ideal of a 'resurgent' Italy was opposed to an Italy controlled and constrained by foreign and domestic 'autocrats'. The growth and success of nationalism in Italy was, and would remain, linked to Great Power rivalry and to political developments outside the peninsula.

The broad outlines of Risorgimento history between 1815 and 1860 are well known. In 1814/15, following the defeat of Napoleon, *ancien régime* Europe and its rulers were 'restored' by the Congress of Vienna. This restoration was, in Italy, strictly defined and controlled by the conservative powers of Europe, and by Austria in particular. Placed under the domination of Metternich's Austria, the restored Italian states reflected the opposition to constitutionalism and the desire to strengthen the moral and political foundations of absolutism that was felt by the conservative powers at the Congress of Vienna. The territorial settlement in Italy reflected also its role as a 'pawn' in international diplomacy and, in particular, its significance to French and Austrian rivalry. The principle of legitimate monarchical right, already challenged by the revolutionary experience, determined the internal political restoration.

By the terms of the Vienna settlement, Lombardy and the former Venetian Republic became part of the Austrian Empire, while the Grand Duchy of Tuscany and the Central Italian Duchies of Modena and Parma were ruled by members of the Austrian royal family (the Habsburg dynasty). The Papal States were returned to the Pope and, in the South, the Kingdom of Naples and the island of Sicily (called the 'Kingdom of the Two Sicilies') were restored to the Bourbon King Ferdinando IV (who became Ferdinando I). Both the Pope and Ferdinando I made concessions to Austrian power in the peninsula. Ferdinando signed a permanent defensive alliance with Austria, which gave Austria the effective right to intervene militarily in the Two Sicilies. The Pope allowed the Austrian army to maintain a permanent garrison in Ferrara. The only Italian state that remained relatively independent of Austria after 1815 was the Kingdom of Sardinia (usually referred to as 'Piedmont' but also comprising Savoy, Liguria and the island of Sardinia). Thanks to its strategic position on the French border, Piedmont served as an independent bulwark between the rival powers of France and Austria, and was actually made stronger by the addition of the Genoese Republic (see Map 1).

The attempt to establish domestic and international political stability through the restoration of pre-revolutionary administrations did not go unopposed. Not only in Italy, but also in France, Spain and the German states, the legitimacy of *ancien régime* governments was challenged by increasingly vocal constitutional and democratic movements. A whole series of revolutionary disturbances took place in Europe between 1820 and 1848. In Italy, relatively minor revolutionary conspiracies and insurrections were usually easily dealt with but, during 1820 and 1821, more major revolutions occurred in Piedmont and the Two Sicilies. A revolutionary conspiracy in Central Italy during 1831 briefly over-threw Papal government in parts of the Legations (the northern region of the Papal States). In 1848–9, a wave of popular revolution in Europe engulfed all the Italian states. These revolutions were eventually defeated too, partly as a result of dissension within the revolutionary movements. Probably the decisive factor, however, was foreign inter-vention since the Austrian army was involved in the repression of the 1820–1, 1831 and the 1848–9 revolutions. Partly as a means of challenging Austrian power and partly in response to domestic (Catholic) pressure, France became involved in the restoration of Papal authority in 1831 and in 1848.

Nevertheless, the revolutions of 1848–9 did mark a turning-point in liberal fortunes. One Italian state, Piedmont, maintained the constitution granted by the king in 1848 and, from then on, its political development diverged markedly from the rest of Italy. Although fairly restricted in terms of its commitment to political change, the Piedmontese constitu-tion guaranteed basic liberal freedoms, such as the freedom of the press and freedom of association and assembly. It also established a parlia-ment, albeit one based on a very narrow suffrage and with limited executive power. Particularly after 1852, when the moderate liberal Count Camillo Cavour became prime minister of Piedmont, parliament began successfully to assert its authority. A series of reforms liberalised the bureaucracy and judiciary and effectively limited the power of the monarch and the Church. Cavour also used parliamentary power to instigate far-reaching economic and financial reform, and to strengthen the position of moderate liberals within the political system. Finally, he used his skills as a diplomatic negotiator to promote the interests and prestige of Piedmont within Europe.

The growing power of moderate liberals in Piedmont, and the notable success of their economic and political reforms, significantly altered the political climate and balance of power within Italy as a whole. Ten years after the defeat of the 1848–9 revolutions, Piedmont fought a successful war against Austria with French assistance. In 1859, the Austrian province of Lombardy was united with Piedmont, although Venetia remained under Austrian control until 1866. In early 1860, the Restoration governments of Tuscany, Parma and Modena were over-thrown, along with papal authority in the Legations, to be replaced by moderate liberal administrations which also declared union with Pied-mont. In the Two Sicilies, the Bourbon monarchy was also overthrown, this time by a popular army led by the democrat Giuseppe Garibaldi who sought to unite Southern Italy with the Northern state of Piedmont. Finally, the Papal States (excluding the area around Rome which was guarded by a French garrison until 1870) fell to the Piedmontese army, which marched south to meet Garibaldi's volunteer army. In March 1861, Vittorio Emanuele II, the king of Piedmont, was declared king of a united Italy (see Map 2). In 1870, following the withdrawal of French troops from Rome, the Italian army occupied the city. Rome finally became the capital of Italy (see Map 3). The Pope, however, maintained an implacable opposition to the new state, proclaiming himself (and his successors) to be a 'prisoner of the Vatican' and ordering Italian Catholics not to participate in politics.

RESTORATION GOVERNMENT

Italy's Restoration governments have traditionally been seen as the embodiment of a doomed attempt to recast the absolutist structures that had been destroyed by the French Revolution. The alliance between the Restoration governments and the Church, and the Restoration alliance with the conservative Austrian Empire add to their reactionary and generally unsympathetic image. The unification of Italy in 1859–60, following the defeat of Austria by Piedmont and France and the internal collapse of the Restoration states, casts an additional shadow of defeat and failure over these governments. As a result of the defeat of Austria in 1859 and the victory of the liberal-national movement, the liberal critique of Restoration government became the official history of the Risorgimento. The political instability, social upheaval and economic problems of the period 1815–60 were explained as a struggle between progress, represented by Italian liberals, and reaction, represented by the Restoration governments. The defeat/collapse of Restoration governments in 1859–60 was attributed to their pursuit of anachronistic economic policies, to their endorsement of clerical obscurantism, to their brutal and ineffective treatment of popular unrest and, above all, to their inability to embody the aspirations and expectations of the resurgent Italian nation.

Even in the Marxist analyses that became popular in the 1950s and 1960s, this liberal interpretation of the Risorgimento in terms of a struggle between progress and reaction had great force. Its advantage lay in how much it could explain: the growth of a liberal movement could be linked to the emergence of a capitalist economy and the rise of industrial society, while the opposition of Restoration governments to liberalism could be linked to the more general resistance of pre-capitalist elements to a change in the mode of production. In this way, the establishment of a united, liberal Italy seemed to be part of a more general epoch of 'bourgeois progress' in Europe, an epoch that produced a political structure more appropriate to the needs of capitalist accumulation.

One consequence of this implicit 'Whiggish' approach to the Italian Risorgimento is that Restoration government has rarely been the main focus of analysis. The liberal movement, the representative of progress, has inevitably played a more significant role in Risorgimento narratives. For example, liberal opinion depicted Restoration Italy as dominated by a conservative alliance of throne and altar which sustained clerical privileges and religious corruption, and the nature of this alliance has often been taken for granted by historians. The repression of popular unrest and the establishment of surveillance networks against the revolutionary threat can, in a similar way, be interpreted as evidence of reactionary attitudes and regressive tendencies.

Risorgimento liberals criticised the economic policies of many Restoration governments, particularly the maintenance of protectionist barriers against foreign goods and the failure to improve the economic infrastructure. Historians have also seen these policies as crucial in explaining the unpopularity of Restoration government. In Lombardy-Venetia, for example, it was argued in liberal circles that the protectionist policies of the Austrian Empire benefited Austria at the expense of local interests. High taxation was also considered to benefit the imperial treasury in Vienna by draining Lombardy-Venetia of its economic resources. The Marxist historian Giorgio Candeloro echoes these views: the wealthy Italian provinces of Lombardy-Venetia were indeed the 'milch cow' of the Austrian Empire, victims of Austrian greed and European indifference.[3] Hence – and Lombardy-Venetia is merely the most visible of a number of cases – economic issues explain the growing power of nationalist feeling in Italy. It also becomes clear why the unification of Italy should be attributed to the inexorable logic of history. Italian unification appears to be part of a broader European trend that saw the decline of multi-national Empires and regional states, and the general consolidation of modern states around an idea of national independence and nationhood.

The starting-point of 'revisionist' studies of Italy's Restoration governments is that this distinction between progress and reaction is unhelpful and unworkable. Out-and-out reaction was only attempted in a few specific places and periods, usually with dubious results. Moreover, recent research has shown that much of the opposition that developed to Restoration government was based, not on frustrated liberal demands, but on resistance to their more 'progressive' and reforming policies, in particular their policy of administrative modernisation. Revisionist historians in Italy have used an analysis of these 'progressive' policies, and of the reasons why the process of reform was ultimately unsuccessful, to establish a new research agenda for the Risorgimento.

In an article on the origins of the Austrian administration of Lombardy-Venetia, written in 1971, Marino Berengo describes accounts of Austrian misgovernment as the 'black myth' of Risorgimento historiography.[4] Berengo's intervention coincided with a growing interest in the structures and forms of Restoration government in Italy, and with a tendency to focus on aspects of Restoration government that did not impact directly on their relations with liberal movements. The teleology of previous approaches to Restoration government, which refer always to the liberal-national outcome of the Risorgimento, has recently come in for a lot of criticism. Paolo Pezzino challenges 'popular' historiographical approaches to the Bourbon government of Southern Italy which consistently neglect the administrative reforms introduced by the Bourbons in Southern Italy. These reforms have not, he argues, 'acquired the status of an independent object of research', nor have the varieties of Restoration government ever been studied in depth.[5]

The shift in emphasis towards Restoration government has led to a reassessment of their policies. Historians of the Risorgimento have begun to adopt an approach towards modern Italian history that emphasises the problems of state formation. They use a model of state formation that describes a process whereby rulers set themselves the tasks of administrative centralisation and modernisation and of establishing effective relations with a rapidly evolving civil society. The previous, and crucial, distinction between progress and reaction has little relevance to this model, and the causal link between socioeconomic change and changes in the political structure is also abandoned. The sources of instability in the 'reactionary' Restoration states – administrative modernisation, relations between centre and periphery and relations between state and civil society – are also the problems of the liberal Italian state. Moreover, these problems were clearly not unique to Italy. The British, French and German states were all destabilised by the rift between state and civil society. In none of these countries were such problems overcome before the middle of the nineteenth century.

Once the problems of Restoration government are seen as part of a more general European experience, then assumptions about their commitment to reaction can also be questioned. For example, the use of police surveillance, censorship and military repression as a way of dealing with popular and political unrest must be seen in a wider,

European context. At least until the middle of the century, censorship and military repression were the norm in the majority of European states; there is, therefore, nothing exceptionally reactionary about Restoration Italy in this respect. The establishment of formal or specialised sur-veillance bodies (specifically, police forces) in Lombardy, Piedmont, the Papal States and the Two Sicilies was a legacy of the Napoleonic era, not of the *ancien régime*. Again, the organisation of such police forces in Italy was paralleled by developments elsewhere in Europe.[6]

A glance at other European economies also throws a different light on the economic performance of Restoration Italy. First, as Chapter 4 indicates more fully, assumptions about Italy's economic 'backward-ness' in the first half of the century involve a set of unrealistic comparisons with industrial Northern Europe. The kind of commercial and technological infrastructure whose absence was so lamented by Italian liberals was rarely to be found anywhere in Europe during this period. On the other hand, the use of high protective tariffs was common to most European states in the early part of the century. It was only in the 1850s that free trade or reciprocal trade agreements became a feature of the more rapidly developing European economies, and made the maintenance of high tariff barriers by Italy's Restoration states look backward and reactionary. Moreover, the use of heavy taxes on consumption to raise revenue, which proved so unpopular in Lombardy-Venetia and the Two Sicilies, was common government policy throughout Europe and met with similar opposition.

In reality, determined attempts at 'reaction' to the French Revolution were confined to specific rulers at specific times, most notably to King Vittorio Emanuele I of Piedmont and to Duke Francesco IV of Modena in the immediate Restoration period, and to Papal rule between 1823 and 1846. It is worth while looking at these cases in detail, since they do indicate the limitations of a reactionary policy. The Restoration govern-ment of Piedmont between 1814 and 1821 is perhaps the most striking example of reaction at work. Alberto Aquarone has described the process whereby, following Vittorio Emanuele I's return to Piedmont in 1814, the King abrogated all Napoleonic legislation and reinstated *ancien régime* legislation with one single decree.[7] Duke Francesco IV took similar measures in Modena. In both these states, a purge of the administrative and judicial personnel, whose numbers had been greatly expanded in the Napoleonic period to include members of the middle classes, was carried out. All the officials who had served in the Napoleonic Kingdom of Italy were dismissed by Francesco IV of Modena, who proceeded to fill the upper echelons of his bureaucracy with members of the old nobility. In Piedmont, Vittorio Emanuele's minister Cerruti restored all the pre-Napoleonic office holders to their posts, using the Savoy court almanac of 1798 as his guide. If an official had died in the interim, he could be replaced by his son. Hereditary privilege thus replaced the Napoleonic criteria of talent and training as the means of accession and promotion to the higher ranks of the bureaucracy. The Piedmontese army, a stronghold of Napoleonic 'new men', was also purged.

The economic and social policies pursued by Vittorio Emanuele's government can also be described as reactionary: internal and external barriers to trade were erected, old trade corporations and guilds were revived and feudal structures such as primogeniture and *fedecommesso* were reintroduced. The old judicial system, with its privileges and special jurisdictions, replaced the Napoleonic codes. The political, as well as the religious, union of throne and altar was re-affirmed. Control of education was handed back to the Church, and the return of the Jesuits was welcomed in both Piedmont and Modena. Eighteenth-century laws against Jews, restricting their property rights and confining them to ghettos, were also reinstated.

Another attempt to return to the *ancien régime* was made in the Papal States after the election to Pope of the arch-reactionary Leone XII in 1823. Leone XII, and his successors Pio VIII and Gregorio XVI, represented the reactionary group known as the 'zealots'. The Church's hold over the bureaucracy, education and culture was tightened during the reign of these Popes. Religious persecution was intensified. A papal encyclical in 1824 condemned all forms of tolerance (*tollerantismo*). Strict censorship was imposed and movements of opposition were repressed using force.[8]

It is significant, however, that in such cases where reactionaries succeeded in determining the direction of policy, their efforts to restore the *ancien régime* generally ended in failure. Political instability, rather than the return to order hoped for in 1815, was the more common outcome. With the exception of 1848–9, when revolutionary disturbances occurred throughout Italy, revolutions occured precisely in those states (Piedmont, Modena, the Papal States) where more reactionary policies had been pursued. In this most basic way, reaction was not a success, exacerbating rather than resolving the gulf with civil society and increasing the isolation of ruling elites.

These attempts at reaction proved counter-productive not only (or even primarily) because of the extent of opposition but also because the dismantling of Napoleonic political structures was virtually self-defeating. The Napoleonic administrations set up in Northern Italy had been designed to guarantee centralised direction and efficient government. By abolishing them, Restoration governments destroyed a vital instrument of power and political control. Aquarone shows, for example, that the eighteenth-century legal and judicial system that Cerruti attempted to restore to Piedmont in 1814 had been on the point of collapse long before the French invasions. Moreover, in purging the army and bureaucracy Cerruti deprived these institutions of their most able men.[9] The dismissal or demotion of Napoleonic officials and army officers also created considerable discontent and led to political agitation.

In fact, elsewhere in Italy, and perhaps most notably in the Austrian kingdom of Lombardy-Venetia, an attempt was made to reconcile absolutist political structures with the need for political innovation. 'Amalgamation' was a policy actively encouraged by Metternich, who consistently sought to prevent reactionaries from coming to power in Italy. Amalgamation consisted of an attempt to combine the eighteenth-century principles of enlightened absolutism with the administrative and political modernisation of the Napoleonic era to create what historians, borrowing a term from Napoleonic France, call 'administrative monarchies'. These administrative monarchies were based on the principle that an efficient, modern bureaucracy and a centralised administration were crucial to the establishment of absolute authority. Many Restoration governments also accepted that economic development was essential to political stability.

After a brief period of reaction during the Restoration of 1814–15, a policy of 'amalgamation' was pursued by Cardinal Consalvi in the Papal States (before the accession of Leone XII in 1823), and by the government ministers Fossombroni in Tuscany and Medici in the Two Sicilies. Encouraged by Metternich, all these ministers attempted to create more uniform and centralised administrations and to take account of revolutionary ideas and innovations. The personnel of the Napoleonic and *ancien régime* administrations was amalgamated in an effort to find the most capable and loyal officials. In Naples in 1815, the Austrian government intervened to block the reactionary policies of the Principe di Canosa and to enforce Medici's policy of conciliation and reform. Consalvi made a strong (if failed) attempt to open up the Papal bureaucracy to lay officials. Other areas of amalgamation included the judicial system and public education. Many states also embarked upon a substantial programme of public works; the governments of Lombardy-Venetia, Tuscany and the Two Sicilies also helped to encourage economic growth in specific regions.

Alan Reinerman has described how, after the revolutionary upheavals of the early 1830s, Metternich again attempted to broaden support for Restoration politics in Italy through what was called 'consultationary monarchy'. First proposed through the European powers' Memorandum of 1831, which pressed for administrative and legal reforms in the Papal States, 'consultationary monarchy' was based on the Austrian system of congregations, already in force in Lombardy-Venetia, Tuscany and Parma. This system was an amalgam of the eighteenth-century Austrian model and the Napoleonic model. Metternich proposed the establishment of a hierarchical system of communal, provincial and central councils with the task of presenting local demands and opinions to the central government.[10] These councils could include new, as well as more established, social and economic interests. They would thus perform a representative function and obviate, Metternich hoped, the need for more formal representative institutions such as elections and parliaments. In this way, 'consultationary monarchy' was a further attempt to modernise political absolutism through internal administrative reform. In Piedmont and the Two Sicilies state councils along the lines proposed by Metternich were established during the 1830s. Following the election of Pope Pio IX in 1846, a state council was established in Rome as well.

Outside Lombardy-Venetia, the two most notable experiments in consultationary monarchy took place in the Papal States (after 1846) and in Piedmont during the reign of Carlo Alberto (1831–49). In the two years between 1846 and 1848, the new Pope Pio IX introduced major administrative changes, granted amnesties to political prisoners, dissolved the special commission in the Legations and relaxed the controls on the press. The anti-Jewish laws were also relaxed. A programme of public works was ordered, measures were taken to relieve the severe famine prevailing in the Papal States and a customs union with Tuscany and Piedmont was concluded. These reforms created great excitement, especially in liberal national circles where the possibility of papal support was given a huge welcome. Interestingly, however, the pace of reform was too fast for Metternich, who found the new Pope 'lacking in all practical sense'.[11]

In the previously 'reactionary' state of Piedmont, a longer and more concerted process of reform was also embarked upon after 1831. The reign of Carlo Alberto has been the subject of an important 'revisionist' study by Narcisso Nada. Nada shows that it was under Carlo Alberto that Napoleonic penal and civil codes were produced, central and local administrations were reformed and the army was reorganised. Moreover, he argues that Carlo Alberto's financial, economic and educational reforms of the 1840s began the process of change that was to transform the Piedmontese economy in the 1850s. A railway line was built by the state between Turin and Genoa, and Piedmont's high tariff barriers were reduced. Feudalism was abolished in Sardinia as part of a fairly substantial package of reforms designed to improve conditions in the island.[12] More generally, during the 1830s and early 1840s, several (unsuccessful) attempts were made to establish an Italian customs union along the lines of the German *Zollverein* and to co-operate over the construction of a 'national' railway network.

Such efforts to maintain a balance between the establishment of absolute authority and the need for reform or 'modernisation' also extended to religion and the Church. Outside the Papal States, few of the Concordats signed between the restored regimes and the Church totally restored the pre-revolutionary powers of the Church or sought to reverse the secularization introduced by Napoleon. In Europe as a whole, according to Owen Chadwick, 'the word *Restoration* bore only a very partial truth in the Roman Catholic Church'.[13] In fact, Chadwick detects the beginning of a split between Church and state in Italy in the changes introduced by Restoration governments, and not simply in the secular policies of Liberal Italy. The Restoration Concordats, however morally conservative and unpopular with liberals, actually confirmed the pre-eminent role of the state in civil society and the end of many clerical privileges. It is, for example, worth noting that after 1815 control of censorship in Lombardy-Venetia and the Two Sicilies was exercised by the state, not by the Church. The 1818 Concordat with Naples abolished clerical immunities and the crown was allowed to nominate all bishops.

THE FAILURE OF ADMINISTRATIVE MONARCHY

A distinction should be made between the more reactionary administrations of a Leone XII or a Vittorio Emanuele I and those administrations, best represented by conservative reformers such as Consalvi in the Papal States or Medici in the Two Sicilies, that attempted to amalgamate tradition and innovation to create administrative monarchies based on a form of modernised absolutism. This distinction suggests there is no single explanation for the collapse of Restoration government in Italy. It suggests, in particular, that previous explanations for the collapse of Restoration government – the persistence of a reactionary alliance with the Church, hostility to economic growth and to new class interests – cannot explain why these attempts at 'amalgamation' failed. In fact, conservative reformers in the Restoration states were undermined, not by their resistance to change, but by their failure to establish an effective middle way between reaction and revolution.

One symptom of the crisis of 'amalgamation' in the Restoration states was the inability of conservative reformers to carry out an effective process of administrative reform. Marco Meriggi argues that the expulsion of Napoleonic 'new men' from the Lombard bureaucracy, and the restriction thereafter of high positions in the administration to members of the aristocracy, greatly increased the unpopularity of the Habsburg regime among the new middle class.[14] He also suggests, however, that the nobility expected far more from Austrian rule. Trying to mediate between middle-class and aristocratic interests, the administration was compromised in the process. The system of congregations, in particular, satisfied neither one class nor the other.[15] Paolo Pezzino shows how, in Sicily, Bourbon attempts at administrative modernisation were undermined by the combined resistance of the bourgeoisie and nobility.[16] According to Franco Rizzi, in parts of the Papal States local power-holders also successfully resisted the administrative initiatives of the central government.[17]

The above examples suggest that administrative reform, by offending both established and new interests, could create as many problems as it solved. It has been recognised for a long time that resentment of central government, and a profound dislike of the privileges and corruption of the Bourbon capital, lay behind the support given to revolution in the Two Sicilies in 1820. The growth of liberal and republican opposition movements in the Legations (against Rome), in Genoa (against Turin) and in Livorno (against Florence) has also often been attributed to a desire for local autonomy. Liberal sentiments and/or class interests played a less important role in the development of opposition movements than regional resentments and administrative tensions between centre and periphery.

The need to maintain territorial integrity constrained and undermined the process of conservative reform. Pezzino suggests that the alliance between bourgeoisie and nobility in some areas of Sicily frustrated economic reform and administrative centralisation.[18] His research indicates that effective political power in the South was retained by local power-holders, who actually strengthened themselves *vis-à-vis* the central government through the incorporation of bourgeois elements and the manipulation of reforming legislation. Thus, despite significant conflicts within communities (which are discussed in the next chapter), what John Davis calls 'the private exercise of public power' remained a prominent feature of political and social development in the South.[19]

All these factors suggest that 'reaction' could be less unpopular than 'modernisation'. The failure to achieve a balance between competing interests is evident in other areas too. For instance, Bourbon land reforms alienated the old nobility without satisfying the demands of the agrarian bourgeoisie. Furthermore, if liberals were offended by the levels of political surveillance, other groups were equally alarmed by the failure of many Restoration states to guarantee law and order, protect property or police the people effectively. In areas of frequent peasant unrest (the Southern and Sicilian *latifundia*, the Venetian plain) local power-holders tended to demand more, rather than less, repression. Once again, however, it is clear that central government responses were undermined by the lack of control over local areas. The work of Pezzino on Sicily and of Lavan on Venetia indicates that these Restoration governments had in common the problem of recruiting loyal and trained personnel to act as police officers or serve in local bureaucracies.

The process of policy implementation in Restoration Italy, whereby the decisions of central governments were carried out by their local representatives, merits far more attention than it has so far received from historians of the Risorgimento. In this process, the role played by inefficient bureaucracies and by a set of unresolved financial crises may well have been more important in destabilising Restoration governments than frustrated demands for liberal reform. Moreover, if the example of Lombardy-Venetia is at all indicative, bureaucratic and financial problems seem to have thwarted the process of decision-making within central government as well. Lavan shows how, in the case of Venetia, debates about reform could become interminable, and how effective action was often frustrated by the lack of adequate information.[20] It is perhaps in this way that the absence of more institutionalised channels of representation (through elections and parliaments), or of a free press, posed the greatest problems. The process of 'consulting' society in Restoration Italy was slow, inefficient and frequently unrepresentative; governments were unable to respond to new economic interests because they did not know what these interests were. The systems of congregations (which were often in practice dominated by the old nobility) seem to have produced excessive bureaucratisation rather than a responsive and modern central administration.

Conservative reformers in the Restoration states were, on the whole, unable to establish a broad consensus for reform. It is also worth noting that they did little to organise their generally strong basis of support amongst the peasantry. Popular counter-revolutionary militias, such as the *calderai* in the Two Sicilies and the centurions in the Papal States, were organised, but they tended to be used by reactionaries rather than by conservative reformers. Reinerman points out that conservative reformers greatly feared popular militias. Any form of popular militia was believed to be unreliable and inherently unstable, a threat to social order and a challenge to the legitimacy of the state.[21]

The tensions between state and civil society created by administrative modernisation also gave rise to conflict within the governments themselves. Both Meriggi's study of the Lombard administration and Lavan's study of Venetia indicate the extent to which conflicts of interest within these administrations undermined the process of reform. Undoubtedly the most crucial factor frustrating reform was the hostility between conservative reformers and reactionaries. For a brief period after the Naples revolution of 1820, the notoriously reactionary Prince of Canosa was made minister of police and led a 'White Terror' against the liberals.[22] Cardinal Consalvi's efforts between 1814 and 1823 to create a more up-to-date administration for the Papal States were attacked by the reactionary zealots led by Severoli and Pacca. After the zealots gained the upper hand with the election of Leone XII to the Papacy, Consalvi was dismissed and his reforms revoked. Even Prospero Balbo's timid attempts at legislative reform in Piedmont during 1819–20 were rejected by an alliance of reactionaries led by the King.

The idea of 'administrative monarchy' was always controversial and never gained widespread acceptance. Despite pressure from the European Powers, Pope Gregorio XVI simply rejected all calls for reform in the Papal States. He refused to open access to the higher posts of the Papal bureaucracy or to consider any reduction in ecclesiastical privileges. At the same time, demands for reform went unsatisfied and pressure for more radical change built up. As a result, conservative reformers in the Papal States and elsewhere found themselves fighting a battle on two fronts: against reactionaries for whom their policies were dangerously radical and against revolutionaries for whom their policies were too timid.[23]

In turn, the economic and social crisis of the mid-1840s overwhelmed the process of conservative reform. After the 1848 revolutions, conservative reformers were marginalised as all the Restoration governments (apart from Piedmont) adopted more reactionary policies. Strict censorship was imposed and more elaborate spy networks were established; many revolutionaries from 1848 were summarily tried and executed. Repression, in this period, destroyed all attempts at amalgamation and compromise. Government efforts to establish systems of economic or commercial co-operation were abandoned.

CONCLUSION

Conservative reformers in the Restoration governments tended to oscillate between old and new, producing a weak and often inconsistent process of reform. The kinds of political compromises they sought were inherently difficult to reach or to implement. Internal conflicts within administrations, the lack of adequate representative structures, unwieldy bureaucracies and tensions between centre and periphery all undermined conservative reform in Restoration Italy.

None of these structural problems, however, can fully explain why conservative reform became untenable. Two additional factors, often neglected by revisionist historians, need to be considered. First, as mentioned above, the social and economic crisis of the 1840s, culminating in the 1848 revolutions, gave the upper hand in the Restoration states to reactionaries. Second, a changing international climate favoured liberal-national movements and undermined the legitimacy of Restoration governments. Restoration Italy did not simply sink under the weight of its internal contradictions but was actually defeated by an international coalition of Powers directly primarily against Austria. This failure (or inability) of Restoration governments to pursue independent and successful foreign policies played a crucial role in their downfall.

Despite all these problems, it is worth noting that one of the governments which had introduced effective reforms before 1848, and which perhaps came closest to the ideal of an 'administrative monarchy', did survive the traumas of 1848–9 and was able to manipulate the international situation to its own advantage. It is in the context of finding a 'middle way' between reform and reaction, of establishing a stable and broadly acceptable process of political and administrative modernisation, that the experience of Piedmont after 1849 is so significant. Piedmont had the advantage, not shared by other Restoration states, of relative independence from Austria and France. This independence gave the government an opportunity (gravely overestimated by Carlo Alberto in 1848–9 but cleverly used by Cavour in the 1850s) to attract nationalist support for the regime through an anti-Austrian foreign policy. In domestic policy too, the Piedmontese government managed to achieve a more permanent degree of institutional stability and bureaucratic modernisation. Since Carlo Alberto's government included many conservative reformers and comparatively few reactionaries, a stable consensus in favour of reform was gradually established. As a result, the programme of reform pursued under Carlo Alberto could be implemented quite rapidly and was able to attract a limited amount of suppport from the middle class and the liberal nobility. Consequently – and this is perhaps the crucial difference between Piedmont and the other Restoration states – the liberal commitment to reform in Piedmont also came to involve a commitment to the Savoy monarchy.

During the 1850s, the Piedmontese prime minister Cavour was able to expand this programme to achieve a new and dynamic 'amalgam' of absolutism and liberalism, one that represented a viable alternative both to Restoration government and to republican nationalism. Like conservative reformers, moderate liberals feared revolutionary violence and believed in establishing a 'middle way' between revolution and reaction. In addition, however, moderate liberals recognised that a constitution that placed legal limits to absolute power, and a parliament that secured effective representation, were essential to establishing an effective and sustainable process of political change. It was precisely this constitutional alternative, embodied by Piedmont, that was able to bring about the downfall of Restoration government elsewhere in Italy. In a sense, it could be argued that Restoration Italy did succeed in reforming itself as liberal Piedmont, which survived to reshape the structures of the rest of the peninsula in its political image.

Conservative reformers in the other Restoration states had also taken on the task of building a modern centralised state with an efficient, loyal bureaucracy and some form of territorial control, but they had not succeeded. They failed because they did not extend representation sufficiently to those segments of society whose support was vital and because they did not establish an independent foreign policy. Under attack from the Left and despised by the Right, faced with economic and territorial difficulties and a growing financial crisis, these conservative reformers proved unequal to the task that faced them. By the 1850s, with their reform programmes in tatters, the Restoration governments had become isolated internationally, unpopular internally and were unable to co-operate with each other.

However, the failure of conservative reform in Italy before 1860 meant that the challenge facing Risorgimento liberals was not simply one of ousting the reactionary 'foes' of liberty and nationhood. Having done this, they also needed to resolve the political contradictions that had overwhelmed the Restoration states. In this sense, the solution of a united Italy was hardly a solution at all. All that Italian liberals had achieved, in reality, was the establishment of a broad but basic consensus in favour of reform. They had still to make firm and stable administrative links between the new state and civil society, find a cohesive basis of social support and assert Italy's independence abroad. They had to overcome the municipal and regional loyalties that had undermined the reforming initiatives of much smaller states before 1860, and they had to build a new set of national institutions as well as a clear sense of national identity. Finally, they had somehow to mend the immensely damaging rift with the Church which was the direct result of national unification. In this way, the internal political struggles that lay at the heart of the Risorgimento were also, and were perhaps most fundamentally, a struggle against the realities of Italy itself.

3   The Risorgimento and Italian society

BOURGEOISIE AND ARISTOCRACY

There is a long tradition that identifies the Italian Risorgimento with both the aspirations and the material interests of the bourgeoisie. In part, this tradition reflects broader historical interpretations that identify the nineteenth century with 'bourgeois progress' and, in part, it reflects political controversies within Italy. A non-political approach to the Risorgimento, which explains national unification in terms of social and economic developments, has much to recommend it. It provides, above all, a point of departure from the idealist traditions of Risorgimento historiography, which stressed the political, military or diplomatic actions of a small elite and underestimated material considerations and constraints. Yet this identification of the Risorgimento with bourgeois revolution suffers from acute definitional problems. Who were the Italian middle classes? How and when did they carry out a 'bourgeois revolution'? For many historians of the Risorgimento working within this framework, the Italian experience can only be explained as a case of 'failed bourgeois revolution', or as a deviation from liberal middle-class norms.

According to Luciano Cafagna, the idea of the Risorgimento as a 'bourgeois revolution' can be traced to an article written in 1890 by Francesco Saverio Merlino.[1] Merlino, an anarchist, argued that the conflict between peasantry and bourgeoisie, and between bourgeoisie and aristocracy, was fundamental to understanding the outcome of national unification in Italy. Later, in the first decades of the twentieth century, a number of historians began to emphasise the role played by economic factors in the Risorgimento. In 1920, Giuseppe Prato published an important study of the economic and social background to Cavour's (and Piedmont's) political success. For Prato, the achievements of moderate liberals in Piedmont could be explained by reference to the formation of a new agrarian bourgeoisie in the years after 1815.[2] In addition, this kind of class analysis began to be used to explain the dualism between Northern and Southern Italy. Raffaele Ciasca, for example, emphasised the internal social barriers to change in the South.[3] The absence of an industrial or commercial bourgeoisie, and the continuing domination of feudal elements, also explained the different political development of Southern Italy in the nineteenth century.

The emergence of this non-political approach to the Risorgimento was strengthened, and also made more controversial, by the publication in 1934 of Kent Greenfield's *Economics and Liberalism in the Risorgimento*. Focusing on Lombardy, Greenfield emphasised the links between economic development and social change, on the one hand, and the spread of liberal-national ideas, on the other.[4] Greenfield's research on Lombardy led him to conclude that the strongest impetus for the Risorgimento in this region came, not from the bourgeoisie, but from landowners and intellectuals who were often aristocrats. For Greenfield, in other words, the Risorgimento was not a bourgeois revolution at all. Lombard merchants and entrepreneurs were, in Greenfield's analysis, fundamentally conservative and wedded to traditional habits. He pointed to their tendency to invest in land, the traditional source of power and status, as evidence for the lack of entrepreneurial activity in Lombardy. These merchants remained, in David Lo Romer's words, 'largely passive in a changing world'.[5]

A pervasive sense of the 'peculiarities' of the Italian bourgeoisie became fundamental to class analyses of the Risorgimento, even to those analyses that rejected Greenfield's approach and emphasised the essentially bourgeois character of the Risorgimento. Studies of the middle class in Central and Southern Italy, published in the post-war period, also found evidence for this tendency to maintain close ties with the land and adopt a hostile attitude to change.

Undoubtedly the most powerful impetus for the idea of the Risorgimento as a 'failed bourgeois revolution' comes from the historical writings of Antonio Gramsci. Gramsci saw a series of weaknesses in the process of unification in Italy, weaknesses that he attributed to the inability of the bourgeoisie to lead a successful revolutionary struggle against the *ancien régime*. 'The Italian bourgeoisie', he wrote, 'was incapable of uniting the people around itself, and this was the cause of its defeat and the interruptions in its development.'[6] The lack of revolutionary leadership by the Italian bourgeoisie meant that the Risorgimento lacked a mass following and, in particular, lacked a following among the largest section of the Italian population – the peasantry. The Risorgimento was, to use Gramsci's term, a 'passive revolution' or a revolution without mass participation. The bourgeoisie in Italy, unlike its counterparts elsewhere in Europe, had not been strong enough to overthrow the existing, feudal order and had, instead, sought a moderate compromise with it.

As a result of the 'passive revolution', bourgeois rule in Italy could not be 'hegemonic' (based on intellectual, cultural or moral leadership) but had instead to rely on 'domination' (on the state's use of coercion). Relations between North and South were also determined by the 'domination' of Piedmont. Gramsci's Italian bourgeoisie was not a successful class. Italy's bourgeois revolution was a failure in comparison to the French Revolution, and political leadership in the Risorgimento was inadequate by comparison to Jacobin leadership in France. If the Jacobins had, as Gramsci puts it, 'created the bourgeois state [and] made the bourgeoisie into the leading, hegemonic class of the nation', Risorgimento revolutionaries had done neither of these things.[7]

Gramsci's analysis of the shortcomings of class struggle and revolutionary leadership in the Risorgimento relies heavily on a model, derived largely from the French Revolution and more indirectly from the British experience of liberal democracy. Although liberal historians disagreed with Gramsci, and followed Greenfield in pointing to the aristocratic presence in Risorgimento politics, a general consensus was reached about the links between social, economic and political change as an explanation of Italy's development in the nineteenth century. The importance of class (whether bourgeoisie, aristocracy or peasantry) and class conflict is implicitly accepted in many historical debates about the nature of the Risorgimento. A class analysis seems to explain the high levels of popular unrest in Italy, both before and after unification. The differences between North and South (whether economic or political) can also be explained using a class analysis.

Gramsci's approach also fits in well with a broader Marxist interpretation that identifies the rise of the European bourgeoisie with the 'dual' economic and political revolution and, specifically, with industrialisation and liberalism. Eric Hobsbawm, the leading proponent of this interpretation, writes that

the bourgeoisie of the third quarter of the nineteenth century was overwhelmingly 'liberal' .... They believed in capitalism, in competitive private enterprise, technology, science and reason. They believed in progress, in a certain amount of representative government, [and] a certain amount of civil rights and liberties.[8]

As such, the failure of the bourgeoisie to rise to power in Italy is placed in the wider context of the failure of the 'dual revolution' there as well. The attractions of this kind of analysis are, as already discussed in the previous chapter, that it appears to explain so much.

However, this identification of the bourgeoisie with capitalism, industrialisation and liberalism and, thus, with the 'dual revolution' in Europe has been steadily eroded in recent years. First, a huge amount of research on the European bourgeoisie has revealed the enormous diversity of bourgeois activities and bourgeois 'types'. The term 'bourgeois' no longer refers merely to economic activity or, in particular, to an involvement with industry. Instead, the term is often used as a definition of status or to describe a set of ideas or cultural norms. In this broader definition of the middle class, far more attention is paid to the role played by the professions, or more generally by the non-business world, in promoting middle-class values or interests. The attention that has been paid to the *petite bourgeoisie* also points to the existence of internal hierarchies and different activities within the ranks of the middle classes. In Italy, the bour-geoisie are now more often referred to as the *ceti medi* or 'middle orders', a category that refers to status rather than to economic function.[9] Equally, it is possible to talk of 'notables' or 'ruling elites' – also non-economic categories and ones that draw no rigid distinction between the aristocracy and the middle orders.

In this context, the anomalous features of the Italian middle classes, such as its tendency to invest in land or to blend with the old aristocracy, no longer seem like anomalies at all. Even the political attitudes and political development of the middle classes in Italy now seem, if anything, to reflect broader trends. As Arno Mayer suggests, the political subordination of the middle class to the aristocracy was characteristic of most European states until the final years of the nineteenth century.[10] In other words, Mayer's analysis suggests a lack of simultaneity between the dual economic and political revolutions. Geoffrey Eley has recently taken this argument one step further and attempted to dismantle the analytical connections between the emerg-ence of bourgeois civil society, the development of industrial capitalism and the establishment of a liberal parliamentary regime. Marxist accounts of the 'dual revolution' (failed or otherwise) have, he argues, confused and conflated these two experiences which, analytically and empirically, should be treated as independent processes.[11]

The proliferation, over the last decade, of studies of the Italian middle classes has reflected, and contributes to, this broader reassessment in European history. Once 'more widely blamed than studied', in John Davis's words, the Italian middle classes have now moved to the centre of historical analysis.[12] The teleology of previous studies, with their focus on the failings of the Italian bourgeoisie and the failure of national unification, has been replaced by an approach that emphasises the breadth and diversity of the Italian 'middle orders' and avoids privileging those groups involved in liberal or nationalist politics. Rather than being assessed in terms of their success or failure as a 'ruling class', the activities of the Italian middle classes are now viewed as part of a much broader process of change and modernisation. In this context, the link between the Italian middle classes and Italian unification seems very tenuous. Furthermore, the continuities in activities, attitudes and behaviour between Risorgimento middle classes and post-unification middle classes seem greatly to outweigh the discontinuities.

An important source of power and status throughout Restoration Italy and, later, in Liberal Italy too, was the state. Marco Meriggi argues that, in the absence of industrialisation, the attempt to establish modern administrative and juridical systems was the most important cause of social change in this period. In Italy, he suggests, a 'humanistic' bourgeoisie made up of different local groups emerged, tied together only by their participation in public institutions.[13] Employment in the bureaucracy was a source of social formation, particularly for university graduates, providing in the long run a basis for professional class formation in Italy.

However, since most of the Restoration states continued to restrict access into the highest ranks of the bureaucracy, arguably more significant employment opportunities were provided by local administrations. Perhaps above all in the Southern Italian provinces and in Sicily, employment in local administration and involvement in local politics provided an important measure of status and social mobility. For the large number of graduates produced by Southern universities, and often for merchants and landowners as well, a position in the local administration was the easiest means of acquiring wealth, status and security. The powers allocated to local administration – the control over taxation, public works, bureaucratic appointments and, crucially, over the partition of common land – offered to those in charge significant opportunities for patronage and for the direct accumulation of private wealth. Giarrizzo shows how the provincial bourgeoisie of Southern Italy was able in this period to establish autonomous sources of power through the exercise of local administrative tasks.[14]

Nor was this purely a Southern phenomenon. The work of Banti and Malatesta on the behaviour of agrarian elites in the Po Valley after unification indicates the extent to which, in the North as well, involvement in local politics was a vital means of establishing networks of power and influence.[15]

Thus, to some extent, political rather than economic change produced social mobility in many parts of Italy. However, revisionist history does not exclude entirely the impact of economic change on social structures but attempts to indicate instead how all these different processes affected each other, focusing often on the local or regional context. Politics and the professions, as well as agriculture, trade and industry, were all overlapping bases for the formation of new elites. The most obvious manifestation of these changes was the transformation of land ownership. The rapid economic decline of the Venetian nobility during the eighteenth century and after, led to the transfer of land on a large scale to merchants, bankers and *rentiers*. In Sicily, a similar crisis amongst the old aristocracy meant that an increasing amount of land was owned by its former rent collectors. The sale of church and common land also increased the amount of land available for purchase. Thus, in commercial centres such as Milan and Turin, and in ports like Livorno and Catania, wealthy merchants bought up this land as a means of acquiring security and status. For similar reasons, rich bureaucrats and lawyers from the major administrative towns also tended to invest widely in property.

Although those who bought land in Venetia and Sicily tended to adopt the traditional practices and social habits of their departed predecessors, this was never invariably the case. Paul Ginsborg argues that the major social distinction that emerged in the Venetian country-side in the early nineteenth century was based, not on class, but on the difference 'between those who were trying to introduce more efficient and often clearly capitalist methods into agriculture and those who were not'.[16] Elsewhere, especially in the silk-growing regions and in Tuscany and Umbria, the new landowners tended to be both more culturally and socially innovative and more economically enterprising. Frequently, however, members of the old nobility were at the forefront of experimentation and innovation. For instance, before becoming involved in liberal politics during the 1840s, both Bettino Ricasoli and Camillo Cavour led attempts to improve production methods on their ancestral estates. Ricasoli also set up road-building schemes and schemes to house and educate the peasants on his land.

During the nineteenth century, and numerous setbacks notwith-standing, these new elites steadily accumulated wealth. Various strategies were adopted in order to build up capital, status and power but probably the most important mechanism – or at least the one that has been most researched by historians – was the family. If land ownership continued in this period to be the most significant measure of wealth, then family ties and inheritance were the means by which this wealth was secured and increased. The reliance on land ownership and the use of kinship structures by the middle classes has been taken by some historians to be evidence of its feudal habits and atavistic attitudes. However, the more recent work of Banti and Malatesta suggests that such apparently traditional practices were often used as a means of promoting specifically middle-class interests.

These kinds of strategies also often provided a means of 'fusing' with old aristocratic families. This process of 'fusion' with the aristocracy is now seen by many historians of the Italian middle classes as an indication of their dynamic and enterprising qualities. It was, above all, in the major cities, where the greatest opportunities for social ties with traditional elites existed, that the process of 'fusion' between aristocracy and middle classes into a broad ruling elite took place most rapidly. Educational, cultural and philanthropic societies, agricultural and scientific organisations, as well as more explicitly economic bodies such as chambers of commerce, were established and attracted an increasingly diverse membership. Anthony Cardoza describes how, by the 1830s, a more cosmopolitan group in Turin (led by Cavour, Salmour, Alfieri and Nigra) had begun to seek open associational networks between the bourgeoisie and the aristocracy. This new associational culture was often explicitly modelled on the examples set by Paris and London.[17] Milan, in particular, developed as a major cultural and intellectual centre at this time and its liveliness led many contemporaries to compare the city to Paris.

In the absence of effective political representation, a parallel public space based on clubs and journals often developed. According to Banti and Meriggi, a 'profound change in the ways in which social space was put to use' occurred.[18] This bourgeois, secular 'public sphere', which developed rapidly during the 1830s and 1840s, revolved around clubs, cafés, theatres and the press, rather than around family, community and the church. It provided opportunities for members of the various elites to meet and mingle in a new environment.

Much research remains to be done on the development of a 'bourgeois' culture in Italy. Very little is known about the process of secularisation or about levels of religiosity among the middle classes. It is clear that in common with most of 'bourgeois' Europe, the new public sphere defined itself partly by whom it excluded. Those who did participate in this wider public space still tended to come from the most privileged sections of the middle classes. On the whole, only wealthy merchants and the most successful professionals joined clubs, participated in scientific societies or socialised with the aristocracy. Members of the *petite bourgeoisie* were excluded entirely from these networks, as were all women, confined as they were to the 'private sphere' of family and home.

Moreover, recent research suggests that levels of mobility and sociability in the public sphere should not be overestimated. Aristocratic resistance could drastically curtail the process of fusion. Studies of smaller towns, such as Parma, Lucca and Pisa, also indicate the extent to which, in the absence of a new middle class, the old elites were able to maintain their monopoly of power and status well into the 1840s and 1850s. Even where the aristocracy had entered a period of long-term economic decline, as in major cities such as Rome and Palermo which experienced little economic or demographic growth, the small middle class was unable to make contacts with the aristocracy. The aristocracy jealously guarded its remaining privileges and power. One hostile observer wrote in 1838 of the 'feudal, corrupt and arrogant' atmosphere in Palermo, while thirty years later another commentator referred disparagingly to the nobility's 'unhealthy obsession' with owning fine carriages.[19]

In many regions, traditional rivalries still prevailed and divided members of the old nobility. At least in some cities (Naples, Turin), a new form of stratification emerged where the most powerful noble families kept themselves socially and culturally apart from both the lesser nobility and the rich middle class. Cardoza's study of gentlemen's clubs in Turin concludes that, despite the efforts of Cavour and others, the old aristocracy and the rich bourgeoisie co-existed side by side, rather than intermingling.[20] Paolo Macry suggests, in his study of Neapolitan aristocratic families, that cultural and ideological distinctions could be maintained even as the aristocracy entered the bourgeois, public world of business and finance. In the private sphere of family and home, the distinction between modern and traditional behaviour, between what was bourgeois and what was noble, could be rigidly maintained. The home became a symbol of lost order, a personal haven, in a rapidly changing and sometimes violent 'public' world.[21]

Different forms of stratification, and the degree of variation between regions and between localities, suggest that general conclusions as to the political implications of all these changes may be hard to reach. The emergence of new public spaces is generally associated with the development of liberal public opinion in Europe, and there is much evidence for this in some Italian cities; but the absence of any research on the political behaviour, in the Risorgimento period, of these newly defined groups makes it difficult to reach firm conclusions.[22] It is well known how the establishment of new administrative institutions in the early Restoration period became the focus of considerable middle-class discontent. In a few notable cases this discontent translated into an active liberal opposition against the existing regimes. As the previous chapter has already noted, the restriction of opportunities for bureaucratic employment by the Austrians in Lombardy-Venetia, and the attempt in Piedmont to purge the army of its liberal elements, gave an important boost to liberal opposition movements in Northern Italy.

In other respects, however, the adjustments of the Restoration period produced more subtle, and more complex, kinds of social and political tensions. These tensions undermined political stability, often by producing conflicts within communities and involving the private dimensions of public power. According to Enrica di Ciommo, one effect of the Bourbon administrative reforms in Southern Italy was to produce unity within communities as they struggled to resist the effect of these changes. Rapidly, however, this solidarity was eroded as new landed and commercial elites competed with the old ruling class for the resources and privileges assigned by the central government.[23] In many parts of the South, these kinds of conflicts exploded into communal violence. Particularly during moments of political turmoil – for example during the revolutions of 1820, 1848 and 1860 – members of the new elites attempted to seize control of the local administration by force. The National Guards, established during the liberal revolutions of 1848 and 1860, were sometimes used as private armies to support or impose rival political claims.

Personal rivalries had direct consequences for the public sphere. Giovanna Fiume shows how, in Sicily, both sides used bandits in order to reinforce their political claims and to protect or increase their property and wealth. Bandits were 'employed' by powerful families to exact revenge on their enemies, to steal cattle and generally to accumulate wealth. In this way, banditry was linked to political and to class interests and became endemic in many rural areas of Sicily. Behind every bandit, it was claimed, 'there was always the figure of a nobleman, a judge, a mayor or a police chief'.[24] This situation produced political instability, violence and more factionalism rather than liberal opposition movements.

It is thus difficult to generalise about the effects of social mobility in Italy in the first half of the nineteenth century. The development of new elites did involve the creation of new economic opportunities and different forms of social interaction. However, this development was not always accompanied by respect for the rule of law, a sense of national identity or a commitment to the principles of liberal political economy. If, at one extreme, the middle orders and aristocracy of Milan mingled and socialised in theatres, clubs and cafés, at the other extreme, in the isolated towns and villages of Western Sicily, competing elites battled against each other, using all the weapons at their disposal. It is, as yet, far from clear why structural change produced elite violence in Sicily and elite sociability in Milan, although Paolo Pezzino has suggested that these differences may owe more to political relationships than to social or cultural tendencies.[25] What is clear is that, in most parts of Italy, liberalism did not go hand in hand with the growth of a more 'bourgeois society'.

THE RURAL AND URBAN POOR

If the identification of the Risorgimento with the interests and aspirations of the bourgeoisie can no longer be sustained, at least directly, then the role played by class conflict also needs to be reassessed. The thrust of much recent research has been to de-emphasise class conflict in the Risorgimento and, in particular, to deny any connection between popular revolt and political attitudes. Moreover, the surge of historical interest over the last two decades in crime and popular disorder suggests, once again, that there was nothing exceptional about Italy in this period. Social problems resulting from rapid urbanisation and escalating rural poverty, along with an apparent rise in crime and the spread of epidemic disease, were common to all European states.

Gramsci argued that the threat of popular revolution so alarmed the Italian bourgeoisie that it led them to seek compromises with the existing order. In turn, as we have already seen, he argued that the lack of a popular revolutionary alliance fatally undermined the bourgeoisie's revolution. Does this analysis explain the character and direction of popular unrest in the Risorgimento? Does the specific nature of its class conflict and class alliances set Italy apart from other European societies? Before we can answer these questions, it is necessary to look at the sources of tensions and dissatisfactions amongst the rural and urban poor.

The growth of 'dangerous classes' in both rural and urban Italy seems to be part of a much broader European trend. The legal and economic reforms of the late eighteenth century, greatly accelerated during the revolutionary and Napoleonic periods, had dramatic social consequences which were initially felt most strongly in the countryside. The dismantling of feudal structures led to changes in the legal title of land and to the growth of new agrarian classes. An important consequence of these changes was the rapid erosion of customary land-use rights enjoyed by the peasantry. In Italy, this process took place very rapidly and can be connected to the spread of peasant disturbances.

Although these land-use rights differed from one agricultural region to another in Italy, they all provided a means by which peasant families could supplement their income from their own meagre plots of land or from salaried work. One of the most important rights was the right to graze livestock on common land. Others included access to a water supply (particularly important in the arid South), to forestry for the collection of dead wood and, in the coastal wetlands, to the marshes for the gathering of straw and canes. These rights, often together with seasonal migration, sustained impoverished rural communities and protected their inhabitants from destitution.

The enclosure of common land and its conversion into leasehold or freehold property, along with the abolition of rights of forage and grazing, led to drastic changes for the Italian peasantry. The erosion of land-use rights often gave rise to a new differentiation within rural communities. In some regions, peasants were able to acquire a part of the leasehold property for themselves. Perhaps most notably in the Piedmontese hill zones, and in other mountainous areas, a class of small peasant proprietors distinct from the poor landless labourers did emerge. Elsewhere, if peasant farmers were able to buy land they lacked the means to make it profitable. Generally illiterate and without any capital to improve their land, these peasants fell rapidly into debt. They were forced to sell to speculators who, in turn, sold to large landed proprietors. Thus, often the most striking effect of these changes was the creation of ever-larger landed estates owned by single proprietors. In areas of intense commercial activity, such as the Lombard plain, a class of proletarianised wage-labourers (*braccianti*) replaced share-cropping farmers.[26]

In the Lombard and Venetian plains, the impact of the loss of land rights led to a dramatic deterioration in the peasantry's economic position. Piero Brunello shows that the decision of the Vienna government in 1839 to declare all uncultivated common land available for private purchase dealt a devastating blow to many rural communities. Particularly affected by this decree, according to Brunello, were the rural poor whose livelihood depended on hunting, fishing and gathering produce from the extensive and uncultivated marshlands on the Venetian coast. Advances in land reclamation and drainage techniques meant that this long-deserted area became attractive to potential investors and was rapidly enclosed, drained and placed under cultivation.[27] In the province of Lazio around Rome, land enclosures disrupted the pattern of transhumance and accentuated the conflict between arable farmers and cattle drovers (*boattieri*). The livelihood of cattle drovers, often a powerful group within Southern *latifondo* communities, was seriously threatened by these changes.[28] Similar tensions can be found through-out the South and in the islands.

On the whole, therefore, although there was an increase in the land under cultivation during this period, the effects were generally disruptive and rarely beneficial to the peasantry. Moreover, the loss of land-use rights was made all the more harmful by the impact of other developments. First, Italy as a whole experienced rapid, if sporadic, population growth in this period which increased pressure on the land. Second, the growing scale of peasant indebtedness paralysed the peasant economy. Since many small peasant landholders and share-croppers were unable to support themselves by themselves, they relied more and more on loans of various kinds to last from harvest to harvest. It appears that many of the newly enriched landowners and their agents demanded far more usurious rates of interest from their peasant debtors than their aristocratic predecessors ever had. As a result, and throughout Italy, peasants became trapped in an endless cycle of poverty and debt repayment from which there was little escape. Government intervention through indirect taxation (salt taxes, grist taxes), stamp duties and military conscription also increased the peasants' economic burden.

The vulnerability of rural communities to economic pressure is also acutely demonstrated by the high incidences of famine as well as by the spread of epidemic and endemic diseases in this period. Between 1814 and 1818, in the mid-1840s and again in 1853, widespread famine decimated the rural population. Cases of pellagra (a disease caused by vitamin deficiency, and specifically by a diet based exclusively on maize, which caused insanity and eventually suicide in its victims) were widespread throughout Italy. The prevalence of malaria in the summer months depopulated some of the most fertile countryside, transforming it into a deadly, impoverished desert. Probably the most feared disease of all, however, was cholera, which swept with devastating force through the cities and rural areas of Italy between 1835 and 1837, in 1849 and again between 1854 and 1855.

The effects of cholera were felt most strongly in the cities and, as such, will be discussed in relation to the urban poor. The extent to which the peasants' response to the deterioration in their economic position can be linked to their participation (or lack of participation) in the Risorgimento is difficult to judge. Evidence of a wider political consciousness can be found, whether in the welcome given by Venetian peasants to the returning Austrians in 1849, or in the oppositional agitation that developed in Lazio in the local bars and *osterie* frequented by 'foreigners'.[29] In particular, the huge increase in land occupations during the revolutionary years of 1848–9, and the welcome given by Sicilian peasants to Garibaldi who, in 1860, promised land to all who joined his army, suggests that a political link between the peasants and the liberal-national leadership could have been established, had the political will existed.

The problem with this approach is that it takes for granted the existence of some national basis for revolutionary action. It ignores the powerful role of the Church in local communities, which were often dominated by the controlling moral, charitable and educational influence of the parish priest. Intense loyalty to the Church, as well as a sense of dynastic loyalty to the head of state, undermined political movements that appealed to the secular 'nation'. It can also be argued that this emphasis on 'failed revolution' fundamentally distorts the community-based character of all social conflicts in this period. Within these communities, notwithstanding the breakdown of traditional heirarchies, the persistence of powerful vertical ties prevented the emergence of clear class conflict. Davis argues that peasant unrest in the South cannot be separated from the economic conflicts between cereal farmers and cattle drovers, or the struggles for control of local administrations.[30] The work of de Clementi, Caffiero and Rizzi on Lazio also indicates that it is impossible to distinguish class conflict from personal loyalties, local schisms, community tensions or even generational conflict.

There was a great deal of resistance at the local level to the encroachment on common land, and an increasing use of direct action (land occupations, public demonstrations). The use of direct action, indicating a breakdown in old, feudal ties of patronage and deference, has also to be seen in the context of general political changes and, above all, in terms of the administrative centralisation and rationalisation which deprived peasants of any effective voice at the communal level. Brunello has studied the petitions drawn up by the Venetian peasantry in protest at the erosion of land-use rights. These petitions suggest a sense of 'moral economy': they appeal to higher authorities, to a sense of community justice and to traditional rights.[31] In Lazio too, the appeal to community justice was common. Attempts were also made to seek redress through the law; de Clementi finds that, when the enclosure movement was accelerated after 1849, cattle drovers conducted searches in local archives to give a legal basis to their claims.[32]

Local issues could become linked to 'national' issues. Franco Rizzi shows how the revolutionary changes in Rome during 1848–9 affected the province of Lazio and how, in his words, 'the advent of the political in the modern sense of the word' affected rural communities.[33] The Roman Republic was, it should be noted, unique among revolutionary governments of this period in its emphasis on the peasantry and on rural areas. The Republican regime also made new demands on the provinces in terms of active participation and service. Rizzi finds that, in some instances, these impositions were resented. Moreover, the organisation of national guards and new administrations accentuated community conflict, often to the detriment of the Republic. In other respects, nevertheless, the political changes in Rome brought about a transformation in the political attitudes and mentalities of local communities. The declaration of the Republic entailed the establishment of new information networks and signified, for rural communities, the right to form new clubs (*circoli*) and associations and to adopt new forms of public behaviour – to sing patriotic songs, organise patriotic festivals and so on.

Since, unfortunately, Rizzi's study is really the only study of its kind in Italy, it is impossible to reach more general conclusions about the forms of interaction between popular culture and political change. His arguments are given added force by de Clementi's study, also on Lazio, which suggests how structures of authority within local communities were transformed by the political changes of the 1840s. The implication of these analyses is that even a failed revolution (such as 1848–9) can establish the conditions for a crisis of traditional authority and lead, in the longer term, to more general political instability. Applied to an analysis of the Risorgimento, these kinds of 'revisionist' arguments suggest reasons for the breakdown of Restoration government. However, since they also show that so much of political and economic change was experienced in local terms, they seem to imply the impossibility of establishing any form of national revolutionary movement.

Attempts to follow Eric Hobsbawm's celebrated, but now widely criticised, interpretation and link banditry with social protest and, thus, with a missed political opportunity have not been particularly successful.[34] Banditry in Italy, like peasant unrest over land, was tied to local conditions rather than to national trends. Neither Brunello's study, nor a shorter study by Paul Ginsborg, finds much evidence for politically motivated or class-conscious activity on the part of the bandits in the Veneto.[35] In the Sicilian example discussed in the previous section, bandits existed mainly in the service of powerful landlords and barons, whereas in much of the Southern mainland bandits were involved in independent activities, such as smuggling and cattle rustling, for their own private gain. Marta Petrusewicz suggests that brigandage in Southern Italy had no political ideology of its own, and that banditry acquired a political direction only as part of the much broader encounter between local communities and the centralising state.[36]

An additional problem with exclusively class-based analyses is that they tend to assume that protest was the only possible outlet for peasant grievances in this period. In fact, one alternative response was to migrate to the towns. Peasant migration was probably the major reason for the rapid growth experienced by cities such as Milan, Turin and Naples, and the creation there of urban 'dangerous classes'. In these cities, casual work sustained (or failed to sustain) a large section of the poorer classes. Throughout the first half of the nineteenth century, Turin attracted not industrial workers but, in Umberto Levra's words, 'seasonal bricklayers, artisans, porters, street peddlers, domestic servants and, above all, a mass of proletarianised peasants' who eked out a marginal existence often dependent on charity and begging.[37] The population of Milan, more of an industrial centre than Turin, also contained a significant portion of casual workers as well as a very high number of shopkeepers and artisans. Even workers in the industrialising textile sector (the bulk of whom were female) were, until the 1850s, usually paid on a part-time basis and did their work from home.

In many respects, the growth of cities such as Milan, Turin and Naples merely continued at an accelerated rate a process that had begun in every major Italian city during the eighteenth century. In the course of the eighteenth century, the population of Turin more than doubled, while in the thirty or so years between the Restoration and the 1848 revolutions Milan's population grew from 139,000 inhabitants to 189,000.[38] In common with many other rapidly expanding cities in Europe at this time, these urban centres lacked either the infrastructure or the employment prospects to support their growing populations. The creation of a 'dangerous class' of casual labourers who lived, according to one contemporary observer, 'in idleness and vagabondage' and constituted 'a permanent danger to social order' has to be understood in this context.[39] The problems of this hungry, marginal class were intensified by economic reforms, such as the abolition of price controls on foodstuffs. Their problems were, in turn, made more visible by the absence, at least until the middle of the century, of any rigid social segregation in housing. The *palazzi* of the rich housed many poor families, and the destitute lived on the streets, intensifying fears among the propertied elites of robbery and food riots.

A substantial proportion of this 'dangerous class' was female. Simonetta Ortaggi Cammarosano describes the migration of married women to Northern and Central Italian cities, often leaving behind a rural life of unmitigated drudgery. In the cities, they found few new opportunities for work. Legally subordinated to men, and discriminated against in terms of education and wages, they tended to take on the most marginal of jobs, often combining domestic service with weaving, needlework and childcare.[40] The growth in infanticide and infant abandonment experienced in this period (the number of infants abandoned in Milan increased five-fold between the 1770s and the 1850s, and in Florence the number grew by 70 per cent during roughly the same period)[41] is a telling indication of the increasing economic pressures on women. Frequently, mothers would place their babies in foundling homes and return, either when better off or when the babies had grown, to retrieve them.

However, as in London, Paris, Portsmouth or Hamburg, by far the most visible 'dangerous' females were prostitutes. Prostitutes were often, but not always, single women from rural areas, seeking to supplement their meagre incomes as servants, launderesses, seamstresses or waitresses. As Mary Gibson shows, the prostitute's public presence, the presence of a 'woman alone' and independent of accepted moral standards, on city streets in Italy raised a host of fears concerning the effects of urbanisation on the moral, sexual, social and physical health of the population.[42] The association of prostitutes with criminals and vagrants intensified anxiety about the growth of a criminal underworld beyond the control of rational, civilised society. Moreover, prostitutes were blamed for the spread of venereal disease, particularly amongst the armed forces, and as such were considered a significant danger to public health.

Besides the perceived spread of crime and disorder in urban areas, disease constituted the major threat to social stability in many towns and cities of Europe. In Italy, urban growth created a speculative boom in property, resulting in the rapid construction of housing that was both unsafe and unsanitary. There were few fire brigades, bad roads and inadequate hospitals. Narrow streets and high buildings, and the absence of green spaces or of a hygenic water supply created ideal conditions for the incubation of disease. Few, if any, towns possessed adequate sanitary facilities. People disposed of their rubbish in the streets which became open sewers, slept in the same damp rooms as their animals and defecated in front of their houses. In the town of Cremona, in Lombardy, the run-off from the local cemetery was found to have contaminated the water supply.[43]

In such conditions, cholera spread with rapid and tragic results. Two thousand people died of cholera in Genoa during 1835, while those who could fled the city (approximately one-third of the population). In 1837, 13,810 died in Naples and 27,000 people, one-sixth of the total population, died of cholera in Palermo.[44] The spread of cholera is also symptomatic of the wider crisis of urban centres in the nineteenth century. Not knowing the cause of the epidemic, and lacking adequate medical facilities, the authorities were unable to prevent its spread. Italian towns as far apart as Genoa, Livorno, Naples and Palermo experienced riots and demonstrations in the years of cholera epidemics. Riots in Palermo during the 1837 cholera epidemic developed into an anti-Bourbon revolt which spread to the surrounding province and, with the participation of many liberals, eventually to Siracusa and Catania. From the 1830s until the 1860s, liberals in the mainland South and Sicily also attempted to use successive cholera epidemics to stir up anti-government feeling amongst the urban poor, playing on a popular myth which attributed the epidemic to deliberate poisoning. Police controls, imposed by the authorities in an attempt to isolate the disease, merely intensified popular resentment.[45]

Towns and cities were at the centre of all the European revolutions between 1820 and 1871, and Italy was no exception. The problems of Italy's cities in this period – rapid population growth accompanied by the spread of disease and the creation of 'dangerous classes' – were broadly the same as those encountered throughout Europe. It is worth emphasising, therefore, that in Italy as in Europe, all the major urban revolts that took place during this period were not apparently based on these 'dangerous classes' at all, but on the craft workers and artisans.

Artisans were behind the successful popular uprisings in Palermo, Milan, Venice, Livorno and Rome in 1848–9. Unfortunately, for reasons that are far from clear, the experiences of artisans and other 'intermediate' classes in the Risorgimento period have hardly been studied at all. Very little is known, for instance, about the participation of artisans in revolutionary organisations such as the National Guards, or about their access to Republican networks. It is, however, possible to speculate about their motives for revolutionary action. In Italy, although perhaps less than in Europe as a whole, markets for artisanal goods were shrinking due to the influx of cheaper, factory-made, products. As early as 1820, artisans acted in Palermo to protect their corporate privileges which were under attack from government legislation, and to maintain their wage differentials which were being eroded by competition from cheap, rural labour. Increasingly, artisans became dependent on supplying the rich with luxury items, or on satisfying a bourgeois craving for aristocratic style, in order to sustain their livelihoods. They were, therefore, particularly vulnerable to economic downturns. Crucially, and in contrast to the marginal 'dangerous classes', they still possessed in their corporate organisations the means to protest against and to disrupt the new 'bourgeois society'.

SOCIAL CONTROL AND CHARITY

The connections between popular revolt and the Risorgimento are thus difficult to establish. Revisionist historians seem to have concluded that attempts to investigate these connections, at least in class terms, are misleading since they assume a set of relations between economic realities and cultural/political attitudes that did not exist. Instead, a number of historians have begun to investigate the ways in which Italian elites responded in other ways to the increase in rural poverty and the intensification of urban unrest. These investigations throw new light on how relations between state and society, and between classes, were conducted and understood in this period. For example, Marzio Barbagli suggests that charitable institutions could reflect, and interact with, the changing problems of urban society. The increase in infant abandonment led, he argues, to a significant increase in the numbers of foundling hospitals which, in turn, may have actually encouraged impoverished mothers to abandon their babies.[46] Additional research has also shown that the numbers of women seeking assistance in refuges rose rapidly, perhaps reflecting their altered position in society.[47]

Studies of the provision of charity also provide a means of investigating the changing relations between Church, state and society. Much of the charitable assistance available – whether through hospitals, refuges, soup kitchens or loans – was offered by the Church, and was one means by which the Church maintained its power within poor communities. However, in some cities the Church's care of the poor was challenged, first by the initiatives of private citizens and, second, by the state itself. In Turin, the changing focus of charitable work and its removal from religious control was reflected most strongly in the development of an independent educational system, at the instigation of its new urban elite. A number of children's schools (*asili infantili*) were established in Piedmont, Tuscany and Naples during the 1840s, with the aim of providing primary instruction for the male children of artisans and the 'labouring' poor. Educational reforms also seem to reflect new bourgeois values. As well as teaching basic literacy skills, an ideal confirmed in the Boncampagni Law (1848) and the Casati Law (1859) in Piedmont, these schools sought to instill values of sobriety, discipline and acceptance of the prevailing social hierarchy.

Stuart Woolf has shown how a vigorous public debate on pauperism developed, which reflected the ideological divisions among elites. Opinion was divided between those who argued in favour of private or religious philanthropy and those who argued for state intervention to solve the crisis. These debates also registered a conflict between approaches to poverty, with Malthusian advocates of liberal self-help taking on proponents of Catholic humanitarianism.[48] In other respects, however, traditional approaches were maintained and, in particular, a distinction continued to be made between the 'deserving poor', those who merited public assistance, and the 'idle poor', the vagrants, beggars and prostitutes from whom society had to be protected. Yet the 'idle poor', too, began to be subject to more unequivocal forms of control and treated in a way that is perhaps recognisably 'modern'.

In this period, according to John Davis, the police acquired new powers of intervention and regulation to deal with the 'idle poor'. For example, in Lombardy, the police were given special powers to prevent the rural poor from entering the towns to beg. The vagrancy law passed in Piedmont in 1829 served a similar purpose. A large number of poorhouses were opened during the 1830s in order to confine those found begging in the towns. Some workhouses, based either on the French or English models, were also established in Piedmont in order to 're-educate' paupers from their supposed indolence by using them for public work projects. Special legislation was passed to deal with the health risk posed by prostitution. From the 1830s onwards, prostitutes in Naples and Palermo were forced to undergo regular medical inspection and, in 1855, a system of licensed brothels was introduced in Piedmont. Under the Piedmontese regulations, those who refused to enter licensed brothels could be arrested, and those found to be suffering from a venereal disease were forced to enter syphilitic asylums.[49]

The establishment of paramilitary rural police forces (*carabinieri*, *gendarmerie*) in most Italian states by the 1830s is also indicative of a preoccupation with rural pauperism and crime. In some respects, the specific criminalisation of brigandage was symptomatic of a broader process, whereby the judicial authorities sought to control and contain the population of rural areas. Bandits were designated as such by the political and judicial authorities, classified as *fuorbandito* ('outlawed') for being a member of an armed gang.[50] In the Two Sicilies, those designated as bandits were condemned to death in their absence, their names were publicly displayed on a list in town squares and highways, and campaigns were mounted to bring them to justice. Bandits thus acquired a unique significance as a symbol of rural lawlessness and as an exceptional threat to civilised society.

The aim of such legislation was to constrain the movement and activity of the 'dangerous' rural and urban poor, and it resulted in increased powers being given to the police. Bandits, vagrants and prostitutes were special categories of criminal, subject to special police controls which, once imposed, were difficult to escape from. In this respect, recent historical research on public order and charity in Restoration Italy reflects a new, Foucauldian interest in social discipline and an emphasis on the 'surveillance' aspects of modern state formation. There is plenty of evidence to show that the poor made no distinction between hospitals, refuges, poor houses and prisons. All were seen as places of confinement or death, while the coercive function of public assistance was recognised and resented.

However, perhaps the most interesting conclusion to be drawn from this research is that, despite the powers allocated to both the providers of charity and the police, much charity and police work was fairly ineffective. The distinction between deserving and idle poor was hard to sustain in the changing environments of Restoration Italy. While the police enjoyed extensive powers they lacked, on the whole, sufficient resources to arrest or confine all those who constituted a 'danger' to society. Although the provision of elementary education did lead, in the long term, to a decline in popular illiteracy, huge disparities remained between North and South and between men and women.

It is also clear, finally, that much of this public assistance and police action was misdirected. The insistence on confining the poor to the countryside was not only impracticable but also indicative of a tendency to romanticise rural life and to ignore real social problems. Police action focused on controlling a 'dangerous class' which was, in reality, more helpless than criminal. Respectable artisans, as the 1848 revolutions showed only too visibly, posed a much graver threat to public order.

CONCLUSION

The complexities of social change in nineteenth-century Italy make it, at least at this stage of historical research, impossible to reach satisfactory conclusions about the relationship of social structures to national unification. In this sense, the Gramscian identification of the Risorgimento with a failed bourgeois revolution cannot be sustained. Gramsci relies on a model of national development that, it seems, fundamentally distorts the locally and regionally based nature of social conflict. Recent research also suggests that his analysis underestimates the problems of creating a revolutionary movement with a truly national appeal. Moreover, Gramsci ignores the dynamic of political action and, thus, the crucial role played by political relationships in the transformation of society. Finally, his notion of 'passive' revolution in Italy relies on a model of successful revolution in France that is highly questionable.

In pointing to the fear of popular revolution and, more generally, to the prevalent social anxiety of this period, a Gramscian analysis still offers important insights. Fear of popular disorder affected the political attitudes of the urban and rural elites. It certainly made them wary of radical change and it clearly bred political discontent. Sporadic riots, robberies and the spectacle of poverty discredited Restoration governments, so apparently unable to enforce public order. Moreover, popular unrest, by adding an extra dimension to existing community conflicts, undermined attempts to modernise government and centralise administrative control.

If it is possible at all to generalise about the political impact of social change, we might, therefore, say that social change produced political instability and that this situation, in turn, undermined the process of state formation in Restoration Italy. In Italy at least, but arguably elsewhere in Europe too, social change in this period produced kinds of political instability to which there were no easy solutions. There was no obvious liberal 'convergence' between the social or economic activities of new elites and the political views adopted by them. Dissatisfaction with government policies did not always translate into active political support for liberal movements. Indeed, demands for local/regional autonomy, fear of popular disorder and a desire for personal aggrandisement often clashed with liberal ideals of national independence, constitutional government and economic progress. It is in this social context that the reversals suffered by liberal-nationalist movements between 1815 and 1860 can be understood. Their successes, on the other hand, would seem to require a different explanation.

4   The Risorgimento and economic development

INTRODUCTION

The economic development of Italy between 1815 and 1860 was a central issue in the liberal critique of Restoration government. Italy's Restoration rulers were restored in 1815 during a period of acute economic crisis. One effect of the revolutionary and Napoleonic wars had been to damage severely Italian trade, along with the economies of the major ports, particularly Venice. A European economic depression undermined agricultural production; many parts of Italy suffered a famine that lasted until 1817–18. The economic reforms of the French period, most notably with regard to infrastructure, lost momentum with the changes of government. A sense of economic decline, and of growing economic weakness relative to their Northern European competitors, dogged Italy's governments up until unification.

This sense of economic 'backwardness' persisted after unification. As a result, a concern with the failure of Italy's economic development in the nineteenth century also came to dominate the agenda of Italy's economic historians. They sought explanations, first, for Italy's late and uneven industrial revolution and, second, for the dualism between North and South which had been such a persistent feature of the Italian economy since unification. As a result, much of the discussion of Italy's Restoration economies was teleological: it sought only to find in the Risorgimento period (and earlier, in many cases) the origins of late industrialisation or of economic dualism in united Italy. The economic literature from the 1950s and 1960s relating to nineteenth-century Italy also belongs to a broader historiography of economic development and the role of state intervention. The economic historian Luciano Cafagna, reflecting on his own research at this time, links his interests to a general post-war concern with the problems of economic growth and with the economic disparities between countries.[1]

These economic questions also had a more general historical significance in that they formed a central element in the debate between
Marxist and liberal historians over the nature of the Risorgimento and
the political achievements of Liberal Italy. The link between weak
economic growth and failed political change, and specifically the link
between the failure of economic unification and political unification,
dominated this debate. At the centre of this debate were two historians,
Emilio Sereni and Rosario Romeo, who concerned themselves with the
economic implications of Gramsci's analysis. Sereni, a Marxist historian, based his account on the theory of 'passive revolution', stressing
the weakness of the Italian bourgeoisie and the slow development of
industrial capitalism. According to Sereni, Italian industrialisation was
retarded by a low level of internal demand, caused by rural poverty and
the propensity of the peasant economy toward self-sufficiency. The
slow industrial growth experienced in Italy could be attributed to
the failure to modernise Southern agriculture (to 'eradicate' feudal
'residues', as Sereni put it), increase peasant consumption and thereby
to create a domestic market for Italian manufactured goods. As such,
Sereni argued, Italy's poor economic performance after 1860 could be
traced to the defeat of peasant revolution in the South at the time of
national unification.[2]

Romeo's starting-point was a rejection of the possibility of peasant
revolution in Southern Italy, which was at the basis of Gramsci's and
Sereni's account. Italy's late industrialisation was, he argued, caused
not by a weak market but by problems involved in the 'original
accumulation of capital' (the increase in the amount of capital offered
for production purposes). Since this 'original accumulation' required
a suppression, rather than an encouragement, of mass consumption
there was, Romeo maintained, an inherent contradiction between
peasant revolution in the South and the development of industrial
capitalism in the North. Industrialisation in Northern Italy (which
took place, according to Romeo, in the 1880s) was only made possible by the Italian state's exertion of fiscal pressure on Southern
agriculture, specifically through the extraction of a surplus from
agriculture which was used to build the administrative and commercial infrastructure necessary for industrialisation to take place. The
political and economic dualisms of united Italy had, in other words,
been crucial to capitalist development; instead of stimulating capitalist
development, an agrarian revolution in the South would have retarded
it still further.[3]

Finally, a challenge was made by the American historian, Alexander
Gerschenkron, to Romeo's account. In a chapter of his book, *Economic*

Backwardness in Historical Perspective, which dealt with Italy as an industrial 'late-comer', Gerschenkron criticised Romeo's 'original accumulation of capital' thesis. Gerschenkron denied any immediate causal link between the extraction of surplus of agriculture and industrialisation, arguing instead that banks, not the state, played the crucial role in investment in industry. The results of state intervention in the economy were, he argued, largely negative; in particular, the protectionist policies pursued after the 1880s probably undermined economic growth. Arguing from a general model that saw industrialisation developing in a series of abrupt 'stages', with a marked discontinuity between stages, he also located the moment of Italy's industrialisation rather later than Romeo, that is, in the late 1890s. The 1890s were, according to Gerschenkron, the period when Italy experienced what he called its big (if in practice rather weak) 'spurt' of self-sustaining economic growth.[4]

It is in the context of these debates about the industrialisation of liberal Italy in the late nineteenth century that the historiography of economic development in the Risorgimento must be seen; and, in this context, a number of methodological features are worth commenting on. First, as Giovanni Federico points out, these models are 'mono-causal', that is, they attribute the character of economic development in Italy to a single cause (the failure of bourgeois revolution, the original accumulation of capital, the action of investment banks).[5] Moreover, the models of the 1950s and 1960s are based on an economic analysis of the political nation; as Sidney Pollard puts it, they assume that 'countries within their political boundaries are the only units within which it is worthwhile to consider the process of industrialisation'.[6] The involvement of national governments in promoting industrialisation is taken for granted, and assessed only on the basis of its relative success or failure. In the Italian context, therefore, the persistence of regional economies and regional governments until well into the nineteenth century had logically to be seen as a major disadvantage.

Underlying all the analyses of Italy's economic backwardness and its position as an industrial late-comer is in fact a sense of the 'peculiarities' of the Italian experience. These peculiarities, it is argued, disadvantaged and weakened Italy's economy *vis-à-vis* its apparently more successful European competitors. In this respect, analyses of Italy's late, uneven or distorted economic development after 1815 are implicitly comparative, at least in the negative sense. They involve an assessment of the Italian economy in terms of what it lacked when compared to economic development in Britain, France or Germany. The absence of heavy industry and the paucity of modern technology, the ruralisation of industrial production and the use of a rural labour force are seen to be key elements of Italy's 'backwardness' in the nineteenth century.

Within the analytical confines of Italy's economic backwardness, attempts were made to isolate specific factors. For example, Italy's late industrialisation was linked to the ruralisation of Italian industries, a process that began in the seventeenth century but was given added impetus in the nineteenth. This process had the effect of delaying the introduction of new technology and the development of factory production. Indeed, it was argued that the ruralisation of industry undermined the competitiveness of Italian manufactured goods to such an extent that it was more profitable to export raw rather than finished materials, even in the case of silk where the Northern Italian climate gave producers a huge natural advantage. Another factor, which related to Italy's 'passive revolution' and was referred to in many Marxist accounts as an explanation for slow economic growth, was the relative absence in Italy of capitalist entrepreneurs. There were, it was argued, few groups in Italy prepared to risk their savings in industrial ventures, new technology or other forms of speculative activity. Instead, merchants throughout Italy tended to invest in land, the traditional source of feudal power and status.

In addition, rural landowners were held responsible for the condition of Italian agriculture, the 'backwardness' of which was often taken for granted. Sereni's arguments about the persistence of feudal relations in Southern agriculture fitted pre-existing notions of Southern landowners as lazy, corrupt and unresponsive to market pressures. The development of commercial agriculture in Lombardy, arguably the most 'capitalist' region in Italy, was, according to Greenfield and others, hampered by absentee landowners and by complex share-cropping contracts that tied peasants to the land.[7] It could be argued that similar contractual arrangements (the *mezzadria*) restricted peasant mobility in Tuscany, thereby maintaining low levels of consumption and preventing more rapid economic growth in the region.

PROTO-INDUSTRIALISATION AND ECONOMIC GROWTH

This image of nineteenth-century Italy as an economically backward, late-industrialising nation, held back by the powerful remnants of a feudal past is, in part, a legacy of Risorgimento rhetoric, sharing with it a sense of conflict between progress and reaction, and between modernity and tradition. Since the 1970s, however, this image, and the economic categories related to it, have been criticised. Perhaps the most important development, in conceptual terms, was the emergence of a model of 'proto-industrialisation' which, although based on analyses of Northern Europe (Saxony in particular), offered new possibilities for studying industrial development in Italy.

The proto-industrialisation model describes and attempts to explain the process, widespread in Europe from the mid-seventeenth to the mid-nineteenth century, whereby industry became established in the country-side and employed the labour of peasant families on a part-time basis. Proto-industrial activity became particularly important in areas of poor agriculture, where peasants were able to use their wages from manufacturing to supplement their meagre incomes from the land. Proto-industrialisation differed from 'cottage' type industry in that goods were produced for distant, sometimes overseas, markets. As such, the model describes a first 'stage' of industrialisation; a mid-point between cottage and factory production. Historians of proto-industrialisation are, however, anxious to stress that the growth of proto-industry was in itself no guarantee of full industrialisation along factory lines. Areas of proto-industrial activity could just as easily fail to develop to the next stage, leading to a process of de-industrialisation.

Although the proto-industrialisation model, with its emphasis on distinct stages in the evolution to full factory production, retains the rigid categories of previous models, it nevertheless suggests far greater complexities in the process of industrialisation. As such, the 'peculiarities' of Italy's economic experiences in the Risorgimento no longer seem quite so peculiar. In particular, the model appears to explain the de-industrialisation experienced in the textile regions of the Centre and South. It also fits the emergence of successful textile industries in Lombardy and elsewhere; Dewerpe has argued that the proto-industrialisation model explains the development of the entire Northern Italian hill zone in this period.[8]

The applicability of the model of proto-industrialisation to Northern Italy suggests that its image as a 'late-industrialiser' is a distorted image. However, the model has itself been much criticised for its assumption that proto-industrialisation can lead only to mass production or to de-industrialisation. Focusing on the Brianza region of Lombardy, Anna Bull finds that the proto-industrialisation model cannot explain the emergence there 'of areas of small-scale industrialisation, as opposed to areas of mass production'.[9] Giorgio Mori suggests that a model of '*pluriattività*', which describes the involvement of peasant families in 'multiple' non-agricultural activities (for example, straw plaiting, mining or weaving) rather than a single proto-industrial activity, is more applicable to many parts of Italy. This pattern of industrial activity, Mori argues, lay behind the diffuse, gradual and uneven process of industrialisation experienced in nineteenth-century Italy. Such diversified, small-scale, rural production should be seen as an effective response to fluctuating world markets rather than evidence of economic 'immobilism' and resistance to technological innovation. This kind of production enabled entrepreneurs to adapt rapidly to changing market conditions, and to take advantage of cheap labour and readily accessible raw materials.[10]

In this context, an alternative view of class relations in the process of economic growth has been offered by some historians. For instance, some evidence of the ability of rural labour to resist the pressures of entrepreneurs is provided by the research of Franco Ramella and Anna Bull. Their research challenges both the Marxist and the proto-industrialisation accounts of the social consequences of industrial-isation (the proletarianisation of the labour force). Bull argues that the sexual division of labour within peasant families, where the male head of the family exploited women's labour, could lead to capital accumu-lation and thus to small-scale ('diffused') entrepreneurship.[11]

The work of Bonelli and Cafagna also broadens the definition of economic growth by challenging the central role of industrialisation in this process. Their model describes the accumulation of a surplus from agriculture over a long time-period, derived from trade and specifically from the export of primary products (silk, cheese). The agricultural surplus provided the impetus for what Cafagna calls a 'pre-industrial' transformation of the Northern Italian economy, which took place after 1820, with diffuse, proto-industrial characteristics and based on artisan production. Much later (after unification), a second wave of indus-trialisation was experienced in Northern Italy, characterised by more concentrated factory production, increased mechanisation and rapid urbanisation. Both historians stress the gradualism of Italy's indus-trialisation; industrialisation can be most accurately depicted as a series of 'waves' rather than a single 'big spurt' or 'take-off'.[12]

If Italian economic growth is interpreted in terms of its basis in agriculture, then it becomes impossible to ignore the crucial role played by silk cultivators and silk merchants. Cafagna writes of an 'industrial–agricultural equilibrium' and of a 'happy relationship' ('*un felice rapporto*') between industry and agriculture, which promoted economic growth in the region. It was through silk exports that Northern Italy became integrated into world markets and its economy was trans-formed. It was, in other words, the revenue generated from the exports of raw and spun silk, particularly in the early nineteenth century when world demand for textiles expanded at an enormous pace, that provided the impetus for the development of banks and credit institutions, which stimulated commercial involvement in industry, which underlay the favourable balance of trade enjoyed by Italy until the 1880s and which, finally, broadened the liberal political agenda to include a discussion of economic interests.[13]

In this new agrarian approach to economic growth in Italy, low levels of internal demand (which permit a balance-of-payments surplus) are seen as a positive advantage and not as a drag on economic growth. Moreover, the continuing (but actually never exclusive) tendency on the part of entrepreneurs and merchants to invest in land, or to locate industrial production in the countryside, is seen in a very different light than before. This kind of behaviour now becomes, as Davis puts it, 'a sign of entrepreneurial rationality rather than an indication of backwardness'.[14]

In a certain sense, the 'Bonelli–Cafagna' model represents an amalgam of various different models, incorporating elements from Sereni and Romeo, from the proto-industrialisation model and from Sidney Pollard's analysis of international trade as a transmitter of industrial technology. Bonelli offers an account of the emergence of capitalism that is multi-causal and attempts to avoid the teleological pitfalls of Romeo's and Sereni's models. He uses a variety of different factors (market structure, the balance of payments, the availability of labour and capital) to explain economic growth in Italy, and to describe it as a more open-ended process. Thus, a feature of the 'Bonelli–Cafagna' model is that it tends to break down the rigid distinctions that characterised previous analyses. The integral part played by agricultural production in the economic transformation of Northern Italy is no longer seen as dysfunctional but axiomatic in explaining the particular pace and character of economic growth. This assessment of Italy's economic performance in the nineteenth century challenges the categories of 'backwardness', and specifically those relating to the backwardness of agriculture.

One final feature of the 'Bonelli–Cafagna' model – its marked emphasis on regions – is worth commenting on. Both Bonelli and Cafagna stress the strong regional variations in patterns of economic growth and analyse the integration of the Northern Italian economy as a region into world markets. In part this reflects a general trend in economic analysis to focus on the crucial role played by regions, and not 'nations' or 'countries', in the construction of world markets. In a sense, therefore, and in striking contrast to the models of Sereni and Romeo, this model makes no claim to describe or explain Italy's economic dualism. Economic dualism is simply taken as a pre-existing given; for Cafagna, 'the development of the North [in the first wave of industrialisation] was in no way conditioned by the existence of a backward South'.[15] This view is echoed by Mori, who describes Italy's restoration economies as 'well and truly distinct', with conflicting interests and far greater trading links with non-Italian states than with each other.[16]

NORTH AND SOUTH

The analytical dissolution of the economic 'nation' into distinct regions, pursuing different kinds of economic development, has far-reaching implications. On the one hand, the 'Bonelli–Cafagna' model, with its emphasis on silk production as the engine of economic growth in Northern Italy, seems to imply a Southern economy left out of the export-led expansion experienced in the North. On the other hand, its insistence on the plurality of paths to economic growth suggests that the Southern economy may merely have been following a separate developmental logic of its own. In recent approaches to the Mezzogiorno, much emphasis has been placed on the different experiences of economic growth. Southern industries were, for example, able to benefit from the Bourbon government's protectionist policies. De Rosa's study of the growth of a modern metallurgical industry in and around Naples indicates how rapidly certain sectors could expand, if protected from foreign competition by high tariff barriers.[17] For similar reasons, some areas of textile production experienced a notable process of techno-logical modernisation and expansion in the early nineteenth century. Thus, the picture of uniform backwardness has to be modified: not all industry in the South was in decline, and not all sectors were experiencing de-industrialisation.

The reassessment of Southern industry has been accompanied by a growing interest in the economies of the major ports, particularly the Sicilian ports. From the work of Iachello and Signorelli on Palermo, Battaglia on Messina and Benigno on Trapani, it appears that the volume of trade in these ports increased rapidly in this period, largely due to an expansion in agricultural exports and other primary products.[18] Benigno refers to the development of a substantial merchant-shipping sector in Trapani in the early nineteenth century, suggesting a local economy capable of innovation and adaptation. The presence, in large numbers, of foreign (British, German) merchants and entrepreneurs in the commercial and industrial centres of the South is well known, and is often taken as evidence for a continuing lack of 'entrepreneurial spirit' among the Southern middle classes. However, Battaglia points to the numerous and varied enterprises that Sicilian merchants were involved in by the middle of the nineteenth century.[19] Arguably, it was only the greater visibility of these foreign entrepreneurs (most famously the Whitakers, Inghams and Woodhouses in Sicily) that obscured the equally important activities of their local counterparts.

It is, however, with regard to Southern agriculture that the most 'revisionist' research has been carried out. The new direction taken by this research challenges a long, and distinguished, historiographical tradition which attributed Southern backwardness to the failure to change and innovate, a failure epitomised by the stagnant condition of its agriculture. From Giustino Fortunato onwards, writers have argued that the 'immobilism' of Southern agriculture was the source of its 'backwardness', that economic development in the South was hampered by the archaic attitudes and traditional practices associated with a rural, feudal past. This economic analysis also concealed a powerful political argument, suggesting that economic 'immobilism' both benefited the particular economic interests and preserved the political privileges of the Southern landowning class. Government intervention in the shape of substantial political and economic reform was seen as the appropriate solution.[20]

This economic and political orthodoxy to which, for example, both Sereni and Romeo responded in different ways, has also recently been challenged. Piero Bevilacqua has stressed the importance of examining the impact of territorial and environmental changes on Southern agriculture. Seen in this light, it can be argued that, at the very least, Southern agriculture was not 'immobile' but was undergoing a process of profound transformation due to the pressure of population on land.[21] The existence within the South of more commercial and dynamic agricultural sectors has also been assigned a far greater significance. Therefore, rather than being isolated exceptions to a pattern of economic immobility, the commercialised agriculture of the 'Terra di Lavoro' near Naples, the 'Conca d'Oro' of Palermo, or the province of Puglia now tends to be seen within the context of more generalised change and economic complexity. According to Franca Assante, the sheer variety of forms of production, types of property and contract, degrees of soil fertility and patterns of demographic settlement, observable both within and between Southern provinces, is the single most striking characteristic of Southern agriculture. Only the most basic distinction, between more dynamic export-led areas and those linked to production for self-sufficiency, is retained in this analysis. 'Every province', Assante writes, 'had its own "South"', its own 'dualisms' between backward and dynamic sectors.[22]

Almost inevitably, revisions of this kind have led historians to reassess hitherto established interpretations of the Southern *latifondo*, the extensive grain-producing estates long associated with backwardness. Marta Petrusewicz, in particular, challenges the more traditional analyses of the Southern *latifondo*, which stress the problems of mono-cultivation and archaic forms of contract. Basing her arguments on detailed research into the private archives of the Baracco estates in Calabria, she suggests that the latifundist estates of the nineteenth century were in fact a specific response to, and in part the creation of, the abolition of feudalism and the development of capitalism in the countryside after the French period. As such, the 'great estates' of the nineteenth century should not be seen as a remnant of feudalism but, more accurately, as a rational variation on a capitalist theme. Instead of economic immobilism, Petrusewicz finds

> a notable elasticity in the latifundist system, which is manifested in the plurality of contractual forms, the variety of judicial institutions, in the notable diversity of crops and, not least, in the coexistence of and interdependence between self-sufficiency and production for trade.[23]

Through the balance between cash crops and self-sufficiency, the latifundist estates were able, at least until the agricultural depression of the 1880s, to adapt rapidly and effectively to changing market conditions. Perhaps even more importantly, the existence of an 'internal market' provided by the peasants and the self-sufficiency of these estates meant that the welfare of peasants was guaranteed. The latifundist estates provided a kind of safety-net against proletarianisation or destitution.

All these revisions to the traditional picture of Southern backwardness have been controversial. The publication of Petrusewicz's *Latifondo* provoked a lively debate; Giancarlo de Vivo argued that she had greatly overestimated the efficiency and paternalism of the latifundist system.[24] Vincenzo Giura has also warned against overestimating the capacity of a 'few isolated valleys' of commercial development to transform the Southern economy.[25]

Perhaps the most serious objection to these revisionist analyses is that they fail adequately to explain the absence of a more general process of economic growth in the South. Petrusewicz attributes the economic decline of the *latifondo* to the agrarian crisis of the 1880s when, she argues, the system was unable to respond to the loss of overseas markets and the fall in grain prices. According to Bevilacqua, the weak political position of Southern Italy hindered the ability of its merchants and entrepreneurs to improve their terms of trade with Northern Europe.[26] Bevilacqua also emphasises the impact of environmental changes and, in particular, the growing land hunger that upset the traditional balance between arable farming and pasture. The increasing percentage of land given over to arable farming and, specifically, the production of corn for export, also entailed a far greater vulnerability to fluctuating world markets. The problems caused by a totally inadequate infrastructure, especially the absence of a modern road network, played a role in hampering economic growth, as did the failure to solve the chronic water shortage and establish an efficient irrigation system.[27]

CONCLUSION

At this point, some readers may be wondering about the relevance of these debates to the Risorgimento and Italian unification. If so, then they will have grasped the central argument of this chapter. The basic thrust of all these explanations, whether the 'Bonelli–Cafagna' model of export-led expansion or Bevilacqua's analysis of environmental factors, is to deny the existence of any straightforward relationship between political developments and economic growth. As such, they challenge the link between economic change and political unification that has been so fundamental to the historical agenda in Italy. With the exception of infrastructural problems, which formed part of the liberal critique of Bourbon government, the other causes of Southern 'backwardness' recently identified by historians – vulnerability to fluctuating world markets, land hunger, the failure to irrigate – were not major political issues, at least not in the Risorgimento period. By far the most important factor affecting all the Italian economies in the nineteenth century was, according to all these explanations, not political (national unification) but their integration into world markets. Moreover, this transformation affected different regions of Italy in different ways and with different results.

It could, in fact, be argued that the only characteristic shared by the Italian economies was a position of relative weakness *vis-à-vis* the 'core' industrialising regions in Britain, France and Germany. Davis argues that the very advantages that cheap labour and low levels of internal demand offered to the Italian producer also proved, in the long run, to be disadvantages. The persistence of a low wage economy greatly assisted exports but also meant that there were few incentives for producers to develop or use new technologies. The lack of internal markets for high-technology products was an additional constraint.[28] The failed attempt, made after national unification, to create national markets probably also damaged Italy's regional economies. On the one hand, the rapid imposition of a national economic policy linked to free trade dealt a damaging blow to Southern industries. On the other hand, and over the longer term, the absence of Italian markets for Lombard silk or for Sicilian citrus fruits meant that these producers were very exposed to the rapid fluctuations of world markets.

Revisionist accounts of Italian economic development in the nineteenth century may ignore the Risorgimento but, obviously, these analyses have profound implications for Risorgimento historiography. They suggest, first, that the liberal critique of the economic policies of Restoration governments was mistaken. The protectionist policies pursued by the Austrian Empire in Lombardy-Venetia and by the Bourbon government in the Two Sicilies were not unpopular, and they seem to have benefited rather than harmed most sectors of the economy. Furthermore, the revisionist emphasis on trade between regions, with world markets as the engine of economic expansion, suggests that there was very little governments could usefully have done to promote economic growth or to cure economic 'backwardness'. Implicitly, in other words, revisionists underplay the role played by liberal governments (most notably the Cavourian administration) in attracting foreign investment, and the role of the unified state in promoting industrialisation.

As such, the revisionist approach to Italian economic history links up with the revisionist approach to Restoration government and to Italian society. Along with a focus on the regional and international constraints to political and economic change, these approaches share a tendency to break down the old, or Risorgimento, distinctions between progress and reaction. Whether in political, social or economic terms, the Restoration governments lacked such a simple choice. Instead, they were faced with the problem of reconciling diverse, and overlapping, local, regional, economic and political interests, without any means of adequately representing them within the government. The failure to formulate coherent economic directives seems to have been the direct result of this problem.

According to revisionist accounts of economic development, the idea of a united Italy was a purely political idea. The economic arguments made by Risorgimento liberals in favour of national unification were, they suggest, mere wishful thinking. Mori refers rather disparagingly to the 'self-conscious and unrelenting drive from minority groups of intellectuals' to create an Italian nation state. Such an objective, he argues, did not figure in the plans of larger and more representative economic groups in Italy at this time, and still less did it figure in the aspirations of the urban and rural poor.[29] According to Cafagna, the establishment of political unity may have been an economic mistake, retarding rather than promoting industrialisation. Moreover, the idea that national unification caused the economic disparities between North and South is seen as a fiction, a fiction that derived from political pressures and struggles for political supremacy.[30]

Why then did national unification take place? How were these unrepresentative, 'minority groups of intellectuals' able to establish an Italian nation state in 1860? It is already apparent, from Chapter 2, that Italian liberals offered little in the way of a radical and coherent solution to the structural and administrative difficulties that undermined Restoration government. Moreover, Italians could, evidently, expect little in the way of material benefits from the creation of a united Italy. Mori suggests that the major factor in national unification was the support given by British and French leaders, who were all anxious to find a way of undermining the power of the Austrian Empire.[31] But this explanation is more valid when applied to the collapse of Restoration government; it fails to account for the viability of a unitary solution within the domestic scene.

It is in this way that the revisionist historiography of the past two decades cannot fully explain the process of national unification. In order to understand why Italian liberals, however impractical their programme and however unrepresentative they were of society at large, were still able to create an entirely different impression of themselves, we need to look elsewhere. Paradoxically, this search leads us right back to a discussion of the political, ideological and emotional appeal of unitary nationalism.

5 The Risorgimento and Italian nationalism

INTRODUCTION

Nationalism in the Risorgimento based itself on an appeal to a unique and glorious past that united Italians and distinguished them from other 'nations'. After political unification in 1860, the Risorgimento itself became part of Italy's common past and provided a form of cultural identity. This shared history, celebrated in Liberal Italy through parades, monuments and popular literature, became more important in defining Italians than a common sense of ethnic or linguistic identity.[1]

Nationalist politics were always the central concern in the history of the Risorgimento, studied in depth long before economic development or social structure became legitimate historical concerns. Studies of personality determined the initial direction of Risorgimento history, which was dominated by the personal reminiscences of prominent liberals.[2] Risorgimento leaders became associated with an ideal of national heroism. Cavour, Vittorio Emanuele II and, above all, Garibaldi, were ranked among the 'Great Men' of the nineteenth century, the 'creators' of Italy and leading proponents of liberty and economic progress. And, as a result of national unification, Italy also became an inspiration to other aspiring 'nations', seeming to confirm that Europe's future stability lay with nation states.

The events of 1859–60, which resulted in national unification and which have always been considered the culmination of the Risorgimento, are well known, and have already been briefly outlined in Chapter 2. However, as we have seen, detailed historical research, inspired in part by a sense of disillusionment with the outcome of the Risorgimento, has long since dented the heroic myths of nationalist historiography. Quite soon after Italian unification, historians of diplomacy identified Cavour (along with the Prussian leader Otto von Bismarck) as the representative of a new 'realistic' approach to politics.

For these historians, Cavour represented a new breed of modern politician willing to manipulate both the international situation and nationalist aspirations to his own advantage.[3]

By the 1950s and early 1960s, a new orthodoxy had emerged in Risorgimento history, which rejected entirely nationalist mythologies and emphasised the elements of *Realpolitik*. Although Denis Mack Smith challenged accounts of Cavour's 'realism', he confirmed the more cynical assessment of Cavour's personality and aims. His book on the relationship between Cavour and Garibaldi in 1860 has the revealing subtitle *A Study in Political Conflict*.[4] For Mack Smith, and other historians influenced by his work, the creation of a united Italy in 1861 reflected the political rivalries rather than the nationalist aspirations of the Risorgimento period. In explaining Italian unification, more attention was paid to analysing dynastic (Piedmontese) aims, political expediency and international rivalry than to celebrating a shared 'Italian' desire for national independence and unity. The war of 1859 was seen as a 'carefully planned accident', in Arnold Blumberg's words, and, as a result of it, ambitious and manipulative politicians had imposed Italian unification from above.[5]

The development of a 'non-political' approach to the Risorgimento, which stressed the impact of long-term economic and social change on Risorgimento politics, also confirmed the negative assessment of Italian unification and the tendency to downgrade the role of nationalism. The Risorgimento was increasingly seen as a movement of (primarily middle-class) elites, with no significant popular support for Italian nationalism. Unification was explained as the outcome of a broader process of change, of a 'dual' economic and political revolution that saw the rise of industrial capitalism and the growth of nation states.

With this approach went a strong emphasis on the rivalries between moderate liberals and Mazzinians. Focusing above all on the 'decade of preparation' for unity (1849–59), historians began also to emphasise the elements of conflict within the Mazzinian movement. Far greater significance was given to the critique of Mazzini from the Left, over his refusal to endorse a federalist and/or a socialist programme. Mazzini's move, during the 1850s, from republicanism to acceptance of a monarchy was interpreted as an abandonment of his principles and a defeat for the democratic movement. According to Alessandro Galante Garrone, Mazzinians were 'tormented and torn by a profound crisis' and began a process of irreversible decline.[6] For Clara Lovett, the experience of political persecution and the loneliness and hardships of political exile were responsible for weakening democratic networks and eroding their support amongst the middle class.[7]

The new or revisionist approach to the 'Risorgimento' (not a term that revisionists favour) does not accept either the nationalist, *Realpolitik* or Marxist explanations of Italian unification. Revisionists are virtually unanimous in rejecting (indeed, ignoring) the nationalist explanation of unification, pointing instead to the persistence of regional and local identities/conflicts in Risorgimento Italy. They also treat the *Realpolitik* explanation with suspicion, associating it with a sense of Italy's 'failure' to live up to an Anglo-Saxon 'norm'. Finally, revisionists take issue with the Marxist assumption of a developmental logic between the rise of capitalism, the growth of a middle class and the political unification of Italy.

The revisionist dissatisfaction with existing explanations of Italian unification manifests itself most clearly in a denial of the central significance of unification itself. Revisionists seek to 'de-privilege' national unification, and to see national unification as only one possible outcome among many. They stress the continuity between the political struggles of Restoration and Liberal Italy, a continuity that can be attributed to conflicts arising from the process of state formation. According to the revisionist account, as we saw in Chapter 2, the modernisation of political and bureaucratic structures by state officials disturbed the established relationships between state and society, both before and after 1860. The breakdown of these relationships (visible in, for example, the growing conflicts between the state and its peripheral territories) was intensified, but not caused, by rapid economic and social change. As such, they suggest that resistance to political or economic change, rather than an unsatisfied desire for it, was responsible for the persistent instability of nineteenth-century Italian politics.

The implications of the revisionist critique are clear. If there were such powerful continuities between state formation during the Restoration and during the Liberal period, and if so much of the social and political instability was caused by local/regional tensions, then national unification can only be explained as an aberration, produced by international power politics rather than by domestic pressure. In this case too, nationalist movements, however vocal, played a clearly subordinate role to the one played by, and between, states. Nationalism, in John Breuilly's words, becomes more important 'as a product than as a cause of national unification'. The 'crucial interventions' in the unification of Italy were made by the leaders of Piedmont, not by nationalist movements.[8]

Implicitly, therefore, the revisionist history of the Risorgimento endorses an account of nationalism that sees it as a consequence, not a cause, of nation-state formation. In practice, however, this account is hard to sustain. Without some reference to the legitimacy of the nationalist solution within Italy before 1860, it is difficult to account either for Cavour's success in manipulating nationalist issues or for the extraordinary – in many ways unprecedented – success of Garibaldi in 1860. It is clear that nationalist movements did not 'create' a united Italy, and that Piedmont did. Yet, nationalism mobilised public opinion against the Restoration states and in favour of Piedmont. The increasing popularity of nationalism (even if only among educated elites) made national unity the obvious political solution after the Restoration states collapsed. Thus, without reference to nationalism, and to what Raymond Grew calls the 'great battle to mobilise public opinion', it is impossible to explain why Cavour was able, or was forced, to unite Italy in 1860.[9]

Although new research has led revisionist historians to abandon the concepts of 'liberal progress' and 'failed bourgeois revolution', it has yet to offer an alternative basis for understanding Italian unification. In order to explain why Italy was unified in 1860, it is also necessary to look at the growth of a sense of national identity before 1860, and at the political impact of nationalist movements. As we shall see, it is very difficult to distinguish, on the basis of cause and effect, between the growing political power of Piedmont within Italy and the growing legitimacy of nationalist ideas. Moreover, the absence of much new work on nationalist politics in this period poses other problems. There are very few recent studies of the links between national identity and nation-state formation, and there is still less work on the links between national identity and popular culture. As a result, my conclusions in this chapter can only be tentative ones.

NATIONALIST POLITICS

There were two main currents of Italian nationalism in the Risorgimento, one political and revolutionary, the other literary and scientific. Both had their roots in the experiences of the revolutionary and Napoleonic occupations, although they could both, arguably, trace their origins to the literary and political traditions of early-modern Italy. Literary and scientific nationalism, based in Northern Italy and associated with a series of journals, newspapers and professional organisations, will be discussed in the next section. Its most significant political influence was on the Northern Italian moderate liberals.

Mazzini was a leading proponent and, to some extent, the creator of political nationalism. He derived his concept of national self-determination from German romanticism and particularly from the writings of Kant and Herder. For Mazzini, nationalism was the new religion for the modern world. Italy, he believed, had been called upon by God to become a nation, and it was only by becoming a nation that it could fulfil its mission as an inspiration for other nations to do the same. Yet, kings and priests, Mazzini insisted, had together corrupted and halted the progress of the Italian nation. Since the institutionalised hierarchies of the Catholic Church had become an obstruction between God and the people, God spoke instead to the people through the collective consciousness of nations. Only a Republic – the 'democratic expression of popular action' – represented and guaranteed the liberty, equality and fraternity of all its citizens.[10]

For Mazzini, individual liberty and national self-determination were both inconceivable without a unitary Republic, and a unitary Republic could only be achieved through popular insurrection. 'Young Italy is unitary', he wrote in his general instructions to this organisation, 'because without unity there is no real nation.' Thus, the most important innovation introduced by Mazzini was the incorporation of romantic nationalism with revolutionary activism and republicanism.[11] Mazzini gave romantic nationalism a concrete political agenda. In his appeal to popular unitary republicanism, he also distinguished his programme from the elitism and sectarianism of the secret societies that had dominated revolutionary politics in Italy before the 1830s.

The success of Mazzini's republican organisation 'Young Italy', which during the 1830s and 1840s gathered enough strength and support to organise a series of uprisings and alarm all of Restoration Italy, lay in its capacity to attract young romantic idealists for whom the idea of individual redemption and a popular war of liberation had a powerful appeal. Moreover, as Paul Ginsborg shows, individual acts of heroism and martyrdom, such as the Bandiera brothers' expedition to Calabria in 1844, could successfully publicise an 'Italian' revolt against monarchical tyranny even if the revolt itself was a total failure.[12] Although these tactics attracted the attention of the police throughout Restoration Italy, and although numerous arrests and failed insurrections blunted the movement's popular appeal, Young Italy was successful in drawing public attention to Italy's 'plight' and in discrediting Restoration government.

Mazzini's greatest moment was, undoubtedly, in 1848–9. Through the revolutionary governments, and most notably through the Constituent Assembly of the Roman Republic, Mazzini was able, if only for a brief time, to give his proposals for a united, republican Italy a concrete form. The defeat of the 1848–9 revolutions in Italy, and the successive defeats suffered by the increasingly divided democratic movement, has tended to overshadow the extent to which the experience of the Roman Republic actually enhanced Mazzini's prestige and political reputation.

In 1848–9, short-term political defeat masked longer-term changes in the growth and appeal of nationalist movements.

An enduring consequence of the revolutions was the development of a nationalist mythology based on its main events and on the personalities involved. The achievements of the Milanese 'five days' of March 1848, Garibaldi's defence of the Roman Republic and the retreat of his army through the Appennines in an attempt to defend Venice against the Austrian siege, were recorded for history as episodes of extraordinary popular heroism. After the defence of the Roman Republic, Garibaldi acquired a unique position as the personification of a national ideal. The scale of his military successes is attributable, in part, to his capacity to inspire personal devotion among his followers. Without his charisma, and without the nationalist enthusiasm of his followers, it is very unlikely that his expedition to Sicily in 1860 could have succeeded.[13]

After the defeats of the 1848–9 revolution, more and more liberals in Italy began to focus on national unity as their primary goal. Before 1848, moderate liberals had tended to be anti-Austrian not pro-Italian; their interest in 'Italy' was confined to history and culture. After the experiences of 1848 these distinctions became difficult to maintain. Even before 1848, many moderates had become enthusiastic supporters of what was called 'Neo-Guelphism', which identified Italian unity with the Roman Catholic Church. The idea of an Italian confederation with the Pope as President, put forward by Vincenzo Gioberti (a Piedmontese priest) in 1843, had to an extent prepared the ground for the moderate espousal of nationalist causes after 1848. Nationalism began to dominate the political agenda after the 1848 revolutions. Mazzinians slowly abandoned their dreams of a unitary Republic in favour of a united Italy in any form, while moderate liberals began to identify economic progress and individual freedoms with a notion of national self-determination.

One important basis for the appeal of nationalism in Italy at this time was that it seemed to offer a simple explanation for Italy's 'failure' – the divisive presence of Austria and of reactionary governments generally, divisions between Italians and between liberals – together with the simple solution of national unity. Thus, in this period and for a broad spectrum of liberal opinion, nationalism came to encompass a whole series of different political demands. As a political ideology, nationalism offered moderate liberals many advantages. In much of Europe, liberal public opinion had begun to promote national self-determination and nation states as the model for political development. Cavour, and other leading moderate liberals such as Ricasoli and

Minghetti, came to see in the language of nationalism a means of emphasising Northern Italy's separate political interests, and pitting them against those of Austria. Specifically for moderate liberals, who were often more interested in economics than in politics, nationalism offered a significant opportunity for promoting the separate economic development of Northern Italy.

Moreover, at this time the international climate appeared to turn against multi-national Empires, as the conservative rulers of Austria and Russia fell out over the war in the Crimea and the French and British governments adopted a more positive attitude towards nationalist movements. Thus, in the international arena particularly, Cavour began to speak on behalf of Piedmont for Italy, and of Italy's oppression by Austria. The prestige that this defence of Italy gave to Piedmont made its king, Vittorio Emanuele II, another late convert to the nationalist cause.

The conversion of Piedmont and of moderate liberals to secular political nationalism radically altered the dynamics of nationalist politics. As many Mazzinians were quick to realise, the moderate espousal of Italian interests gave the nationalist movement a unique opportunity. For the first time, a political group in power was prepared to promote nationalist issues, even if only on an occasional basis and in terms that emphasised Italian independence rather than unity. As a result of Cavour's activities in the 1850s, nationalism acquired far greater respectability and became associated with political stability rather than with revolutionary upheaval.

The 'profound crisis' of Mazzinianism after 1849, and its decline as a political force, can thus be placed in a different context. National unity, the primary objective of most Mazzinians after 1849, did become a reality in 1860. Through Garibaldi's actions in 1860, the Piedmontese moderate liberals were forced to go beyond their original intentions of expelling Austria from Northern Italy and were forced to unite Northern Italy with the South. By 1860, national unity seemed the only and obvious solution to Italy's political crisis. The Venetian democrat, Daniele Manin, had commented in 1857, 'give us unity and we will get all the rest.'[14] The problem was that (and here the Marxist analysis is still very helpful) by 1860 the democratic movement had no institutional or popular base from which to challenge the moderate liberals or to push the democratic revolution forward. The movement itself was demoralised by the apparent setbacks of the 1850s. Mazzinians achieved their main aim in 1860 but lacked either a programme or the power to carry this achievement any further.

Apart from a brief moment in 1860 when the success of Garibaldi's expedition to Sicily led to a surge of popular support for a united Italy, the democratic movement was unable to unite ordinary Italians behind its ideal of national unity. United Italy was the creation of kings, not of the people. However, the inability of the democratic movement to unite the people also made the task facing the moderates much more difficult. The moderates found nationalism a powerful tool in opposition but far less effective as a means of reconciling the disparate elements of Italian society. Moreover, if 1848–9 had converted the moderates to political nationalism, it had turned the Papacy against it for the foreseeable future. Thus, an additional effect of 1848–9 was to destroy the hope of reconciling Roman Catholicism and Italian nationalism. As such, the moderate liberals' espousal of secular unitary nationalism led to a rift between moderate liberals and the Church. In the event, the establishment of national unity proved to be extremely divisive.

THE GROWTH OF NATIONALIST OPINION

A distinction needs to be made between, on the one hand, the impact of a nationalist discourse on Risorgimento politics and, on the other, the political impact of nationalist movements. In a study of the cultural origins of the 1848 revolutions in the South, Enrica di Ciommo argues that the growth of a nationalist discourse before 1848 had a powerful effect on the broader terms in which this revolution was experienced and interpreted. To focus only on revolutionary activities obscures the cultural consequences of revolutionary conflict.[15] In this respect, nationalism could influence the course of political events even where the nationalist movements themselves failed to seize political power.

The presence of Italian nationalism was felt well before the revolutions of 1848–9 transformed nationalist politics. Many historians trace the growth of a sense of *italianità* to the eighteenth century and/or to the revolutionary and Napoleonic period. Franco della Peruta has shown, for example, how soldiers' experiences between 1796 and 1814 emphasised a sense of national consciousness and 'belonging'. In Italy as a whole at this time, the use of symbols such as the tricolour flag appealed to a nascent national identity.[16]

The growth of a sense of *italianità* is also one of the most striking aspects of developments in the visual arts and literature, in the press and in the activities of scientific and economic associations during this period. From the eighteenth century onwards, romantic nationalism pervaded the visual arts. Representations of Italy's past often conveyed a powerful political message, a message that was deliberately placed in a historical context in order to avoid censorship.[17] During the revolutionary and Napoleonic period, the romantic tragedies of Cesare Alfieri and the poetry of Ugo Foscolo also invoked a cultural (linguistic) sense of nationhood and national identity long before these became legitimate political concerns.[18]

The revolt of intellectuals against Restoration government was a powerful factor in the development of opposition movements after 1815. This discontent, due partly to the closing of employment opportunities in state bureaucracies and partly to press censorship, rapidly acquired a national, and nationalist, significance.[19] According to Adrian Lyttleton, 'it was communication rather than the production and exchange of material goods which was most severely hindered by the existing system of states.'[20] Professional literary men writing for a market, and those involved in the book trade itself, had thus much to gain from the establishment of a less particularist, larger Italian culture.

In the course of the eighteenth century, Italy's common past had been 'discovered' by journalists and publishers. After the Restoration, a large number of new literary groups and publishing ventures were established in Northern and Central Italy, and these too were centred around explorations and discussions of Italian history and literature. Many literary publications, most notably *Il Conciliatore* in Lombardy and *L'Antologia* in Tuscany, rapidly acquired a political, oppositional edge and played a crucial role in the development of nationalist ideas and in the growth of nationalist networks. Before 1848, it was primarily through newspapers and journals that both the revolutionary activism of Mazzini and the economic federalism of Carlo Cattaneo became what Angelica Gernert calls a 'programme of action'. Cavour's first experience of politics was through his editorship of the newspaper *Il Risorgimento* in the 1840s.[21]

The coming together of liberal public opinion around an idea of nationhood can also be observed in economic and scientific circles. From the 1830s onwards, liberal agrarian associations in individual Restoration states began to seek contact with each other on a 'national' scale. During the 1840s, a series of scientific congresses were held that gathered scientists from all over Italy and addressed scientific questions in 'national' terms. Sylvana Patriarca shows how an enthusiasm for statistical analysis among educated elites also shaped liberal perceptions of the Italian nation. Statistical representations of Italy were, she argues, 'a clear rhetorical weapon in the hands of the Italian patriots and reformers', constituting a 'precise political statement about the legitimacy and viability of the future nation'.[22]

The revolutions of 1848–9 were a watershed in the development of a nationalist culture in Italy. Piedmont's liberalisation of the press laws and the laws concerning public assembly in 1848 established a whole new, and more public, focus for nationalist activity. It is in this respect that the organisation of the Italian National Society is so significant. Set up in 1857 by the democrats Daniele Manin and Giorgio Pallavicino in order to promote nationalist ideas, and aimed particularly at Piedmontese moderates, the National Society raised money, organised public meetings and produced newspapers to publicise the nationalist cause.

The National Society played a vital role in giving the nationalist cause in Italy a base among the educated middle class. The organisation of the National Society also marks an important transformation in the political discourse of Italian nationalism, away from the language of revolutionary conspiracy and popular insurrection toward the respectability of 'public' parliamentary and journalistic debate. Its leaders persuaded Cavour that a useful nationalist alternative to revolutionary Republicanism existed. By 1860, as Grew shows, the National Society's influence dominated liberal circles in Central Italy, and it was instrumental in winning middle-class support for union with Piedmont-Lombardy.[23] The National Society was largely responsible for organising the plebiscites in Central Italy which voted for union with the North. Moreover, Garibaldi's expedition to Sicily was made possible, at least in part, by money raised by the National Society in Piedmont, Lombardy and the Central Italian Duchies.[24]

In an explanation of why Italy was unified in 1860, the growing political hegemony of Piedmont within Italy cannot be effectively distinguished from the increasing popularity of cultural nationalism or from the growth of a nationalist political culture. If, however, the relationship between national unification and elite culture seems undeniable, the same cannot be said for popular culture. Since nationalism was, before 1860, a movement confined to an urban literate elite, its links with the rest of the population, particularly the rural population, are difficult to explore in any detail. It seems clear that, in so far as nationalist ideas evoked a strong popular response, this response was found in the major cities. There is, for example, evidence of popular engagement with nationalist issues in Rome, Milan and Venice during the 1848–9 revolutions, perhaps because the presence there of foreign (Austrian or French) armies made these issues more immediately relevant. Even in these cases, however, little is known about the 'view from below' – about the forms of popular response or about participation in voluntary organisations.

Recent research stresses the community basis of political conflict in rural Italy and questions the possibility of any identification between community and nation. According to Lyttleton, Italian democrats never succeeded in overcoming the gap between city and countryside. The Church's opposition to Mazzini's secular religion considerably blunted its popular appeal. His anti-clericalism alienated the rural clergy, who were such an important factor elsewhere in winning peasant support for the nationalist cause. Moreover, Lyttleton argues that the interest in rural life and folk culture, 'so strong a component of many nineteenth-century nationalisms', was largely absent in Italy.[25]

In this way, historical analysis of the links between Risorgimento ideals and popular culture focuses on what was missing: Italian nationalist movements had no interest in rural life, and the peasantry had no interest in nationalism. This implies that there is, in effect, no history of popular culture in the Risorgimento to write about. However, some new research suggests that political events and new ideas could have a powerful impact on rural communities, even if their results were not always those intended. In particular, the work of Rizzi and de Clementi on the impact of revolutionary change in the Roman province of Lazio suggests that even short-term and failed revolutionary change could have a long-term effect on the structure of power in local communities. The advent of the Roman Republic in 1849 may, they suggest, have radically altered peasant attitudes to authority and to the Papal regime. It gave rise to generational conflict and challenged established hierarchies, as well as emphasising pre-existing community divisions. The formation of popular clubs and political organisations in the *osterie* and *caffé* of Lazio also signals an important transformation in political behaviour and a growing awareness of 'national' issues.[26]

There is, perhaps, another way in which the relationship between popular culture and Risorgimento ideals could be explored, which might also throw a different light on the activities of nationalist movements. Historians' embarrassment at what Raymond Grew describes as 'the miraculous stories, pseudo-Baptisms and adulation surrounding Risorgimento heroes' has meant that the relationship of these representations to popular culture has never been studied in depth.[27] However, the use which Italian nationalists made of religious symbolism, and their appeal to religious values, may explain one element of the popular response to Garibaldi. According to Grew, Garibaldi's ability (and the more limited ability of other Risorgimento heroes) to mobilise popular opinion owes much to their endorsement of popular religious feelings. Grew defines these feelings as the 'common operative values of fairness, dignity and social order' and this seems to have been precisely what Garibaldi (briefly) offered to the Sicilian peasantry in 1860.[28] In this way, a study of religion and popular beliefs in the Risorgimento might well open up new perspectives on the relationship between political leadership and popular culture. By confronting the nationalist myths of the Risorgimento, instead of trying to ignore them, it may yet be possible to write the history of popular culture in the Risorgimento.

CONCLUSION

The slow development of a national culture in Italy, and the growth of a nationalist discourse among educated elites, strongly influenced both the nature and the outcome of the crisis in 1859–60. National unification, in this respect, is not at all difficult to explain. In both Italy and in Europe, one of the great strengths of nationalism was its capacity to appeal on different levels to different groups. Nationalism gave meaning to diverse opposition movements and to the diffuse resentment felt towards Restoration governments. Both Mazzinians and moderates could find in nationalist discourse a justification for their political beliefs and actions. Using the political language of nationhood, Mazzinians and moderates were able to present their programmes as the embodiment of liberty and progress, and their aims as a set of self-evident, unavoidable national imperatives.

Yet, the very factors that made nationalism unstoppable by 1860 also created great difficulties. Notwithstanding the claims made by its supporters, national unity was a political and cultural aspiration, not a historical inevitability. There was little agreement about how the Italian nation should be defined. Romantic representations of nationhood had nothing in common with the scientific descriptions of statisticians. The secular message of Italian nationalism clashed with the unifying beliefs and customs of the Catholic Church. The 'national' interests of moderate liberals lay with a separate union of Northern Italy, and with a reformed political system controlled by an enlightened elite that would bring about material progress. Mazzinians, by contrast, identified the nation with popular sovereignty, and with an ideal of unitary republicanism and revolution that thoroughly alarmed moderate liberals.

For Italian elites, 'nationalism' was often a euphemism for 'regionalism'; their sense of *patria* could also be defined in local terms. Enthusiasm for nationalist ideas masked the resentment felt by Palermo liberals towards Naples, and the jealousy between Tuscan and Piedmontese reformers. The members of middle-class circles who read nationalist newspapers and participated in National Society debates in Northern and Central Italy cared little, if at all, for the demands of Sicilian peasants who saw Garibaldi as their personal saviour.

The political, diplomatic and economic disappointments of Italian unity, which fuelled the increasingly bitter political struggle after 1860, will be discussed in the concluding chapter. Behind these disappointments, however, lay a deeper dissatisfaction with nationalism itself. Although a consciousness of national identity developed with the establishment of a new, public sphere, this public sphere excluded all but the most wealthy and literate. As such, national identity was defined very narrowly. Not only the poor and illiterate but all women, whose role in the Risorgimento was defined by Mazzini as that of 'mother, sister and wife', were excluded from legitimate participation in this new national public sphere. At the same time, the steadfast opposition of the Church challenged the unitary appeal of nationalism and provided an alternative source of cultural identity.

In all these respects, nationalism offered no permanent basis around which Italians (or Sicilians, Tuscans or Venetians) could unite, and no coherent political alternative to Italy's disintegrating Restoration governments. The events of 1859–60, accompanied as they were by a foreign war, institutional collapse and popular upheaval, greatly intensified the same rivalries, conflicts and tensions that had led to political instability in the first place. It is thus hardly surprising that the Mazzinian formulation of national unity and self-determination, which made Italy for the next sixty years such an example and inspiration to other aspiring 'nations', proved incapable of satisfying anybody in the country of its birth.

6   National unification and the 'post-Risorgimento'

ITALIAN 'PECULIARITIES'

The experiences of Liberal Italy in the 'post-Risorgimento' were in fact a disappointment to many. The 'poetry of the Risorgimento', in Charles Delzell's words, 'gave way to the prose of the post-Risorgimento'.[1] The failure immediately to include Venetia and Rome within the unitary state seemed a particularly striking admission of national weakness. Rome was an especially potent symbol of Italian unity and strength, and its absence from Liberal Italy was felt very acutely. Rome only became part of Italy in 1870, when defeat in the Franco-Prussian war forced Napoleon III to withdraw the French garrison from Rome. The price was a lasting breach between Church and state. Pope Pio IX withdrew as a self-proclaimed 'prisoner' into the Vatican, and a papal encyclical threatened Catholics with excommunication if they participated in Italian politics. Venetia was won from the Austrians earlier, in 1866, but only after a humiliating defeat by the Austrian navy had served to emphasise Italy's lack of independence and power. Other Italian regions, most notably the Trentino (or South Tyrol), remained 'unredeemed' until after the First World War.

Liberal Italy experienced other immediate difficulties in the first few decades of national government. Popular unrest did not cease with the collapse of the Restoration states. The explosion of rural banditry in the South and urban riots in Turin and Milan created severe public-order crises throughout the 1860s. During the war against Austria in 1866, anti-government rebels occupied the city of Palermo and held it for a week in defiance of government authority. During the 1870s, parts of Central and Southern Italy became major strongholds of anarchist activity.

These problems can also be seen against the background of a financial crisis and slow economic growth. The growing budget deficit led to a convertibility crisis in 1866 and to the decision in 1868 to reinstate the *macinato* (grist) tax, an unpopular tax associated with the *ancien régime*. The expected benefits of free trade were slow to materialise too, bringing prosperity to areas of commercial agriculture but dealing a sometimes devastating blow to manufacturing industry, particularly in the South.

Political life in Liberal Italy was also a source of dissatisfaction. The decision, made by Cavour and emphasised by his successors, to 'piedmontise' all existing administrative institutions and, thereby, to impose a centralised political structure on the rest of Italy, was unpopular in most of the former states. It served to emphasise rather than undermine regional rivalries and local resistance. Centralisation was accompanied by a parliamentary system based on a narrow suffrage (2 per cent of the population) and by a repressive policy towards popular unrest that seemed to be little different from the practices of the *ancien régime*.

Underlying all these problems was the more long-term failure of the new state to embody national unity, to establish political consensus or (the most spectacular failure of all) to unify the wealthy, urban North with the impoverished, rural South. At the time, members of the Left opposition in the Italian parliament (former Mazzinians, radicals and federalists) emphasised these problems and pointed to the evidence of failed 'resurgence'. These sentiments were echoed in later historical debates. In Marxist analyses, the shortcomings of liberal Italy were explained by reference to the failures of national unification and the Risorgimento. The 'passive' nature of Italy's revolution had led, it was argued, to a weak bourgeois hegemony and, hence, to the reliance on coercion rather than popular consent as a basis for government. The economic 'backwardness' of Liberal Italy was also attributed to this passive revolution and, specifically, to the failure to eradicate feudal residues and allow commercial relations of production to penetrate the countryside.

One great attraction of this approach was how much it explained. It suggested that Italy's economic and political development in the nineteenth century had a single, discernible pattern. The experiences of Liberal Italy, its failure to develop as a full parliamentary democracy and, thus, its eventual collapse into fascism, could be traced back to the process of national unification and to the struggles of the Risorgimento. In this way, Italy's unique experience in the nineteenth century (no other 'nation' had a 'risorgimento') accounted for its 'peculiar' development in the twentieth century.

More recently, many historians have come to criticise the assumptions underlying this approach. Revisionist historians question Marxist

definitions of class as an economic category and they question the role
assigned to class in political change. Most revisionist research on social
change in nineteenth-century Italy implicitly rejects the identification
of the Risorgimento with a failed bourgeois revolution. Revisionist
historians also question assumptions as to the inevitable downfall of
Restoration government in Italy, and emphasise instead the modernising
aspects of these regimes. They adopt an approach towards political and
economic change in nineteenth-century Italy that challenges the teleological focus of previous accounts, and attempts to avoid reducing
assessments of modernisation to single categories such as class or
nation. Finally, revisionists have sought to abandon notions of the
'peculiarities' of Italy's development which are inherent not only in the
Marxist explanation of a failed Risorgimento, but even in the concept of
a Risorgimento itself.

By focusing on the continuities between Restoration and Liberal Italy,
revisionists are able to illuminate the 'peculiar' features of political
change in nineteenth-century Italy. They also place this change in
a broader context. Through an emphasis on the modernising process of
state formation, the political instability that was such an enduring
feature of nineteenth-century Italy can be explained, but in a way that
avoids reducing this experience to its outcome (national unity, industrialisation, fascism). The revisionist description of state formation in
nineteenth-century Italy centres on a set of relationships (state–society,
centre–periphery, church–state), and argues that what altered these
relationships, and caused so much upheaval, was not so much economic
change as changes in the way in which political power was conceived
and exercised. National unification, as we have seen, was one result of
the crisis caused by these political changes.

Seen from a comparative perspective, three factors distinguish the
Italian experience of state formation from the British, French or
German cases in this period – the general failure of internal reform
before 1860 (Piedmont is a partial exception), the scale of the political
crisis in 1859–60 and the subsequent failure to overcome regional
barriers to 'nation-building'. These factors seem to account both for the
collapse of the Restoration states in 1859–60 and for the political
instability of Liberal Italy.

Italy's 'peculiarities', such as they are, can be partially explained by
the greater vulnerability of the Restoration states to international
pressure. Between 1815 and 1860, Italy's political destiny was to a
considerable extent decided by statesmen in Vienna, Paris and London.
Austrian protection after 1815 meant that the fortunes of Italy's
Restoration states rose and fell with Austria. Thus, until the defeat of

Austria in 1859, the Restoration states could for the most part ignore internal pressure for political change. With the defeat of Austria, this pressure became overwhelming. After 1860, foreign policy considerations, and specifically the necessity of demonstrating the integrity and viability of the new state to the European powers, influenced the decision rapidly to unify Italy's administrative structures and to repress popular and political unrest.[2]

The problem of maintaining territorial integrity also seems to have been far more acute in Italy than elsewhere. Karl Wegert suggests that the experience of state formation in the nineteenth century was far easier, and far more tranquil, in smaller, more compact states such as those of South-West Germany.[3] In Italy, local, elite-led resistance to administrative modernisation challenged the territorial integrity of many states. Most notably in the Two Sicilies and the Papal States, this resistance undermined the process of internal reform. Thus, the threat of internal disintegration contributed to the crisis of Restoration government. In view of the outcome of the events of 1859–60, it is not surprising that after 1860 the same problem of maintaining territorial control persisted. Local and regional resistance to the new central power after 1860 frustrated the process of bureaucratic modernisation and undermined efforts to construct a sense of national identity.[4]

The hostile attitude of the Church to united Italy further weakened both the state's legitimacy and its interventionary power. The Church's attitude, and the physical presence of the Pope in Italy, perhaps accounts for the greatest 'peculiarity' of the Italian experience. Although the struggle between Church and state was a prominent feature of nation-state formation in France and Germany, only in Italy was the Church's temporal power under threat. In this respect, and in striking contrast to political nationalism in Ireland and in parts of Eastern Europe (arguably the 'nations' most affected by the Italian experience), Italian nationalism after 1848 was set on a collision course with the Catholic Church. The collision, which came about with national unification, emphasised the 'national' power of the Church and the fragility of the secular 'Italian' state.

When Pope Pio IX obliged Italians to choose between their loyalty to the Church and their support of the new state, he dealt a devastating blow to the legitimacy of Liberal Italy. Pio IX, unlike the new state, possessed both the moral and the institutional power to enforce his instructions. The beliefs, rituals and language of the Catholic Church united Italians, as Gioberti had noted in the 1840s, in ways that a sense of secular nationhood did not. In the overwhelming majority of cases, the Church's control of education and charity also gave priests a hold over local politics that the liberal state, for all its claim to represent a new bureaucratic authority, could not even aspire to.

A REVISIONIST RISORGIMENTO?

By emphasising the changes brought about by state formation in nineteenth-century Italy, the new revisionist approach lends itself to a comparative rather than a national-specific analysis. In this respect, it represents a radical and innovative departure from previous historiographical traditions in Italy and reflects, more broadly, a revised understanding of the role of the state in European modernisation. It also attempts to challenge the teleology of previous approaches that linked the process of 'Risorgimento' to that of national unification and to fascism.

This challenge to teleology, which again reflects wider changes in nineteenth-century historiography, is quite controversial. John Breuilly (referring to trends in German rather than Italian historiography) has suggested that teleology – 'the understanding of events and situations in relation to what comes afterwards' – is an essential part of historical explanation; 'knowing what comes next' is, indeed, the 'one advantage the historian enjoys over the historical actors'. He argues that the only alternative to a teleological approach is a historicist one, based on the argument that 'every historical case must be understood on its terms, and for its own sake'. For Breuilly, the historicist approach is untenable and incoherent, representing an abandonment of the attempt to understand general processes of change over time.[5]

Although Breuilly expresses the unease felt by many historians, this rejection of a middle way between historicism, on the one hand, and teleology, on the other, seems to be somewhat misplaced. The neat patterns established by historians in an attempt to understand general processes over time can be quite misleading, whereas a more open-ended analysis can actually clarify the different experiences of change and modernisation. In any case, the revisionist critique of teleology in modern Italian historiography does not represent anything quite as drastic as Breuilly suggests. To an extent, Italian historians have circumvented the problem of historicism by substituting 'state formation' for 'Risorgimento'. State formation is conceived as a process with a variety of possible outcomes, of which only one is nation-state formation. Moreover, behind the revisionist challenge to teleology lies a distinct research agenda: to account for the uneven spatial and temporal aspects of modernisation and to bring out the different ways in which it was experienced.

Ultimately, at the centre of the revisionist agenda is a drive to abandon the whole idea of a 'Risorgimento', now seen merely as the product of a nineteenth-century myth that stressed a common Italian past.[6] The Risorgimento, the ideological expression of a cultural and political minority, is thus divorced from the process of national unification. State formation, not the aspirations and misconceptions of Italian nationalists, determined political change in nineteenth-century Italy.

The revisionist critique of the teleology of 'Risorgimento' has undoubtedly led to a new, vigorous and stimulating approach to nineteenth-century Italy. However, as a result of this new research, it has become very difficult for historians to explain why national unification ever took place in Italy. The process of state formation may explain aspects of the 'modernising' process, and it seems to account for the political instability of early nineteenth-century Italy. What it cannot explain is national unification. National unification was far from the obvious solution to the crisis of Restoration Italy in 1859–60. Indeed, since this crisis can in part be attributed to the fear rulers had of territorial disintegration, then the disadvantages of creating a much larger, more unwieldy state should have been obvious to everyone.

As such, the appeal of a myth of 'resurgence' through national unity cannot be ignored. National unification was seen as a solution in 1859–60 since by then it seemed, however mistakenly, to be a historical inevitability. In this respect, the misjudgements of contemporaries tell us more than historians, with the benefit of hindsight, can reveal. Moreover, historical interest in the Risorgimento also reflects the growing legitimacy of nationalism as a solution to political crisis. If a tension between what was, and what might have been, determined historical debate, this tension reflects political struggle in the years before unification. A sense of Italy's future possibilities, and a dissatisfaction with its present state, dominated liberal discourse and political opposition in this period. Historical narratives, with their emphasis on turbulent events, flamboyant personalities and clearly identifiable villains are, in a sense, the product of nationalist demands. Even Marxist analyses, by stressing the disastrous consequences of a failed revolution, respond to the disappointment of the democratic movement in the years after 1848.

The link between the Risorgimento and national unification may ultimately prove difficult to break. No other European 'nation' had a 'Risorgimento' and none described these experiences in such vivid, romantic terms. The revisionist approach to state formation, with its emphasis on identifiable structural change, neglects the relationship of political change to Risorgimento ideals. As Raymond Grew points out, clichés have content; myths and stereotypes are also a form of historical evidence.[7] In order to deconstruct national myths, we have first to understand their meaning and impact. In order to explain why the process of state formation in Italy resulted in national unification, it is necessary to refer to the emotional and political appeal of nationalism. The 'poetry of the Risorgimento', and the potency of this unique national myth, may have blinded nationalists to the powerful divisions within Italian society but the drive for national unity and/or independence significantly altered the outcome of state formation. The 'poetry of the Risorgimento' may not explain the 'prose of the post-Risorgimento', and it does not account for the process of change in nineteenth-century Italy. It can, however, provide crucial insights into the ways in which this change was explained, experienced and acted upon.

Notes

THE RISORGIMENTO AND ITALIAN HISTORY

1 R. Drake, *Byzantium for Rome: The Politics of Nostalgia in Umbertian Italy* (Chapel Hill, 1981), N. Bufalino, 'Giuseppe Garibaldi and Liberal Italy: History, Politics and Nostalgia, 1861–1915' (University of California at Berkeley, Ph.D. thesis, 1991).
2 B. Croce, *Storia d'Italia dal 1871 al 1915* (Bari, 1928), published in English as *A History of Italy, 1871–1915*, trans. C. M. Ady (Oxford, 1929), A. Gramsci, *Il risorgimento* (Turin, 1949). Extracts from Gramsci's Risorgimento writings are published in *Selections from the Prison Notebooks of Antonio Gramsci*, ed. and trans. Q. Hoare and G. Nowell Smith (London, 1971).
3 F. Chabod, 'Croce storico', *Rivista Storica Italiana*, 64, 1952, pp. 473–530.
4 Croce, *History of Italy*, p. 5.
5 Gramsci, *Selections from Prison Notebooks*, pp. 118–19.
6 F. della Peruta, *I democratici e la rivoluzione italiana* (Milan, 1958), *Mazzini e i rivoluzionari italiani* (Milan, 1974). For further discussion of these issues, see P. Ginsborg, 'Gramsci and the era of bourgeois revolution in Italy', in J. A. Davis (ed.), *Gramsci and Italy's Passive Revolution* (London, 1979).
7 R. Romeo, *Dal Piemonte sabaudo al Italia liberale* (Turin, 1963), p. 128.
8 G. Luzzato, 'La vigilia e l'indomani dell'unità italiana', in *Orientamenti per la storia d'Italia nel risorgimento* (Bari, 1952).
9 R. Romeo, *Risorgimento e capitalismo* (Bari, 1959).
10 The derogatory meaning of the term 'reactionary', and its relationship to its opposite, 'progressive', are discussed in A. O. Hischmann, *The Rhetoric of Reaction. Perversity, Futility, Jeopardy* (Cambridge, Mass., 1991), pp. 8–10.
11 See especially D. Mack Smith, *Cavour and Garibaldi, 1860: A Study in Political Conflict* (Cambridge, 2nd edn, 1985) and *Italy. A Modern History* (Ann Arbor, 1959)
12 Mack Smith, *Cavour and Garibaldi*, p. 1.
13 Mack Smith writes of the response in Italy to his work in the preface to the 1985 edition of *Cavour and Garibaldi*.
14 A.W. Salomone (ed.), *Italy from the Risorgimento to Fascism. An Inquiry into the Origins of the Totalitarian State* (New York, 1970). See also H.

Stuart Hughes, 'The aftermath of the Risorgimento in four successive interpretations', *American Historical Review*, 61, 1955, pp. 70–6.

15 G. M. Trevelyan, *Garibaldi's Defence of the Roman Republic* (London, 1907), *Garibaldi and the Thousand* (London, 1909), *Garibaldi and the Making of Italy* (London, 1911).

16 P. Macry, *Ottocento. Famiglia, élites e patrimoni a Napoli* (Turin, 1988), p. x.

17 ibid., p. ix.

18 M. Meriggi, 'Fiscalità e cultura materiale nel Lombardo-Veneto', *Quaderni Storici*, 74, 1990, p. 473.

19 F. Rizzi, *La coccarde e le campane. Comunità rurali e repubblica romana nel Lazio (1848–1849)* (Milan, 1989), p. 230.

20 A. M. Banti, *Terra e denaro. Una borghesia padana dell'ottocento* (Venice, 1989).

21 P. Bevilacqua, *Breve storia dell'Italia meridionale dall'ottocento a oggi* (Rome, 1993), p. viii.

22 D. Blackbourn and G. Eley, *The Peculiarities of German History* (Oxford, 1984).

23 G. Eley, 'Liberalism, Europe and the bourgeoisie 1860–1914', in D. Blackbourn and R. J. Evans (eds), *The German Bourgeoisie* (London, 1991). For an application of his remarks to Italy, see L. Riall, 'Elite resistance to state formation: the case of Italy', in M. Fulbrook (ed.), *National Histories and European History* (London, 1993).

24 A. J. Mayer, *The Persistence of the Old Regime. Europe to the Great War* (London, 1981).

25 M. Meriggi, *Amministrazione e classi sociali nel Lombardo-Veneto 1814–1848* (Bologna, 1983), and *Il regno Lombardo-Veneto* (Turin, 1987).

26 N. Nada, *Dallo stato assoluto allo stato costituzionale. Storia del regno di Carlo Alberto dal 1831 al 1848* (Turin, 1980).

27 For a useful discussion of this approach, relating to Germany, see J. Breuilly, 'The national idea in modern German history', in J. Breuilly (ed.), *The State of Germany. The National Idea in the Making, Unmaking and Remaking of a Modern Nation-State* (London, 1992).

28 See, however, Ginsborg, 'Gramsci and the era of bourgeois revolution'.

29 J. Davis, 'Remapping Italy's path to the twentieth century', *Journal of Modern History*, forthcoming, 1994.

30 R. Romanelli, 'Il comando impossibile: la natura del progetto liberale di governo', in *Il comando impossibile. Stato e società nell'Italia liberale* (Bologna, 1988).

31 R. J. M. Olson, 'In the dawn of Italy', in R. J. M. Olson (ed.), *Ottocento. Romanticism and Revolution in 19th Century Italian Painting* (New York, 1992), A. Finocchi, 'Arte e storia', in *Risorgimento. Mito e realtà* (Milan, 1992).

32 D. Lavan, 'Studies in the Habsburg Administration of Venetia, 1814–1835' (Cambridge University, Ph.D. thesis, 1991), p. 6.

33 S. J. Woolf, *A History of Italy 1700–1860. The Social Constraints of Political Change* (London, 1979), D. Beales, *The Risorgimento and the Unification of Italy* (London, 2nd edn, 1981), H. Hearder, *Italy in the Age of the Risorgimento, 1790–1870* (London, 1983), F. Coppa, *The Origins of the Italian Wars of Independence* (London, 1992).

2 THE RISORGIMENTO AND RESTORATION GOVERNMENT

1 A. Scirocco, 'L'amministrazione civile: istituzioni, funzionari, carriere', in A. Massafra (ed.), *Il mezzogiorno preunitario. Economia, società e istituzioni* (Bari, 1988).

2 J. A. Davis, '1799: the "Santafede" and the crisis of the "ancien regime" in Southern Italy', in J. A. Davis and P. Ginsborg (eds), *Society and Politics in the Age of the Risorgimento. Essays in Honour of Denis Mack Smith* (Cambridge, 1991), p. 3.

3 G. Candeloro, *Storia dell'Italia moderna,* vol. 2, *Dalla restaurazione alla rivoluzione nazionale* (Milan, 1958), p. 23.

4 M. Berengo, 'Le origini del Lombardo-Veneto', *Rivista Storica Italiana,* 83, 1971, p. 544.

5 P. Pezzino, 'Monarchia amministrativa ed *élites* locali: Naro nella prima metà dell'ottocento', in *Un paradiso abitato dai diavoli. Società, élites, istituzioni nel mezzogiorno contemporaneo* (Milan, 1992), pp. 98–101. The economic policies of the Bourbon government have been studied in depth by John Davis, *Merchants, Monopolists and Contractors. A Study of Economic Activity and Society in Bourbon Naples, 1815–60* (New York, 1981).

6 C. Emsley, *Policing and its Context, 1750–1870* (London, 1983).

7 A. Aquarone, 'La politica legislativa della restaurazione nel regno di Sardegna', *Bolletino Storico Bibliografico Subalpino,* 57, 1959, pp. 21–50, 322–59.

8 M. Caravale and A. Caracciolo, *Lo Stato Pontificio da Martino V a Pio X* (Turin, 1978), pp. 606–12.

9 Aquarone, 'La politica legislativa', pp. 29–30, 43–44.

10 A. J. Reinerman, *Austria and the Papacy in the Age of Metternich,* vol. II, *Revolution and Reaction 1830–1838* (Washington, DC, 1989), pp. 35–80.

11 F. J. Coppa, *Cardinal Giacomo Antonelli and Papal Politics in European Affairs* (Albany, 1990), p. 45.

12 N. Nada, *Dallo stato assoluto allo stato costituzionale. Storia del regno di Carlo Alberto dal 1831 al 1848* (Turin, 1980).

13 O. Chadwick, *The Popes and European Revolution* (Oxford, 1981), p. 538.

14 M. Meriggi, *Amministrazione e classi sociale nel Lombardo-Veneto 1814–1848,* (Bologna, 1983), pp. 201–47. David Lavan's research suggests, however, that even this kind of opposition to the Austrian administration (at least in Venetia) has been overestimated: 'Studies in the Habsburg Administration of Venetia, 1814–1835' (Cambridge University, Ph.D. thesis, 1991), pp. 308–66.

15 Meriggi, *Il Regno Lombardo-Veneto* (Turin, 1987), pp. 42–51, 78–83, 93–4.

16 Pezzino, 'Monarchia amministrativa ed *élites* locali', pp. 159–76.

17 F. Rizzi, 'Pourquoi obéir a l'état? Une communauté rurale du Latium aux XVIIIe et XIXe siècles', *Etudes Rurales,* 101–2, 1986, p. 279.

18 Pezzino, 'Monarchia amministrativa ed *élites* locali', p. 175.

19 J. A. Davis, 'The Napoleonic era in Southern Italy: an ambiguous legacy?', *Proceedings of the British Academy,* 80, 1993, p. 148.

20 Lavan, 'Studies in the Habsburg Administration of Venetia', esp. pp. 83–126.

21 A. J. Reinerman, 'The failure of popular counter-revolution in

Risorgimento Italy: the case of the centurions, 1831–1847', *The Historical Journal*, 34, 1991, pp. 21–41.
22 C. Cingari, *Mezzogiorno e risorgimento. La restaurazione a Napoli dal 1821 al 1830* (Bari, 1970), pp. 14–100.
23 Reinerman, *Austria and the Papacy*, vol. II, p. 1.

3 THE RISORGIMENTO AND ITALIAN SOCIETY

1 L. Cafagna, 'Se il risorgimento italiano sia stato una "rivoluzione borghese"', in *Dualismo e sviluppo nella storia d'Italia* (Venice, 1989), p. 161.
2 G. Prato, *Fatti e dottrine economiche alla vigilia del '48. L'Associazione Agraria Subalpina e il conte di Cavour* (Turin, 1920).
3 R. Ciasca, *L'origine del Programma per l'Opinione Nazionale del 1847–1848* (Milan, 1916).
4 K. R. Greenfield, *Economics and Liberalism in the Risorgimento. A Study of Nationalism in Lombardy, 1814–1848* (Baltimore, 1934).
5 D. Lo Romer, *Merchants and Reform in Livorno, 1814–1868* (Berkeley, 1987), p. 5.
6 *Selections from the Prison Notebooks of Antonio Gramsci*, ed. and trans. Q. Hoare and G. Nowell Smith (London, 1971), p. 53.
7 ibid., p. 79.
8 E. J. Hobsbawm, *The Age of Capital, 1848–1875* (London, 1975), p. 287.
9 A. Lyttleton, 'The middle classes in Liberal Italy', in J. A. Davis and P. Ginsborg (eds), *Society and Politics in the Age of the Risorgimento* (Cambridge, 1991), p. 218.
10 A. J. Mayer, *The Persistence of the Old Regime. Europe to the Great War* (London, 1981) pp. 129–87.
11 G. Eley, 'Liberalism, Europe and the bourgeoisie 1860–1914', in D. Blackbourn and R.J. Evans (eds), *The German Bourgeoisie* (London, 1991).
12 J. A. Davis, 'Remapping Italy's path to the twentieth century', *Journal of Modern History*, forthcoming, 1994.
13 M. Meriggi, 'La borghesia italiana', in J. Kocka (ed.), *Borghesie europee dell'ottocento* (Venice, 1989), pp. 165–6, 175.
14 G. Giarrizzo, 'Borghesie e "provincia" nel mezzogiorno durante la restaurazione', in *Atti del 3 Convegno di Studi sul Risorgimento in Puglia. L'età della restaurazione (1815–1830)* (Bari, 1983).
15 A. M. Banti, *Terra e denaro. Una borghesia padana dell'ottocento* (Venice, 1989), M. Malatesta, *I signori della terra. L'organizzazione degli interessi agrari padani (1860–1914)*, (Milan, 1989).
16 P. Ginsborg, *Daniele Manin and the Venetian Revolution of 1848–49* (Cambridge, 1979), p. 15.
17 A. Cardoza, 'Tra caste e classe: clubs maschile dell'élite torinese, 1840–1914', *Quaderni Storici*, 77, 1991, pp. 364–6.
18 A. M. Banti and M. Meriggi, 'Élites e associazioni nell'Italia dell'ottocento: premessa' *Quaderni Storici*, 77, 1991, p. 358.
19 Quoted in O. Cancila, 'Palermo', in *Le città capitale degli stati pre-unitari. Atti del LIII Congresso del Istituto per la Storia del Risorgimento Italiano. 1986* (Rome, 1988), pp. 288, 291.

20 Cardoza, 'Tra caste e classe', p. 385.

21 P. Macry, *Ottocento. Famiglia, élites e patrimoni a Napoli* (Turin, 1988), pp. xiii–xv, 259–62.

22 Marco Meriggi considers the public activities of Milanese elites in an important new study, *Milano borghese. Circoli ed élites nell'ottocento* (Venice, 1993).

23 E. di Ciommo, 'Élites provinciali e potere borbonico: note per una ricerca comparata', in A. Massafra (ed.), *Il mezzogiorno preunitario. Economia, società e istituzioni* (Bari, 1988), pp. 967–8.

24 G. Fiume, 'Bandits, violence and the organisation of power in Sicily in the early nineteenth century', in Davis and Ginsborg (eds), *Society and Politics in the Age of the Risorgimento*, p. 84.

25 P. Pezzino, 'Introduzione: la modernizzazione violenta', in *Una certa reciprocità di favori. Mafia e modernizzazione violenta nella Sicilia postunitaria* (Milan, 1990).

26 Greenfield, *Economics and Liberalism in the Risorgimento*, pp. 30–1, Ginsborg, *Daniele Manin and the Venetian Revolution*, p. 23.

27 P. Brunello, *Ribelli, questuanti e banditi. Proteste contadine in Veneto e in Fruili, 1814–1866* (Venice, 1981), pp. 15–17, 102–4.

28 A. de Clementi, *Vivere nel latifondo. Le comunità della Campagna laziale fra '700 e '800* (Milan, 1989), M. Caffiero, 'Usi e abusi: comunità rurali e difesa dell'economia tradizionale nello stato pontificio', *Passato e Presente*, 24, 1990, pp. 73–93.

29 F. Rizzi, *La coccarde e le campane. Comunità rurali e repubblica romana nel Lazio (1848–1849)* (Milan, 1989).

30 J. A. Davis, *Conflict and Control. Law and Order in Nineteenth Century Italy* (London, 1988), pp. 43–5.

31 Brunello, *Ribelli, questuanti e banditi*, pp. 28–9.

32 De Clementi, *Vivere nel latifondo*, p. 214.

33 F. Rizzi, *La coccarde e le campane*. p.20.

34 E. Hobsbawm, *Bandits* (Harmondsworth, 2nd edn, 1985).

35 P. Ginsborg, 'After the revolution: bandits on the plains of the Po 1848–54', in Davis and Ginsborg (eds), *Society and Politics in the Age of the Risorgimento*.

36 M. Petrusewicz, 'Society against the state: peasant brigandage in Southern Italy', *Criminal Justice History*, 8, 1987, pp. 1–20.

37 U. Levra, *L'altro volto di Torino risorgimentale, 1814–1848* (Turin, 1989), p. 48.

38 S. J. Woolf, 'Segregazione sociale e attività politica nelle città italiane, 1815–1848', in E. Sori (ed.), *Città e controllo sociale in Italia tra XVIII e XIX secolo* (Milan, 1982), p. 22.

39 M. Gibson, *Prostitution and the State in Liberal Italy* (New Brunswick, 1986), p. 16.

40 S. Ortaggi Cammarosano, 'Labouring women in Northern and Central Italy in the nineteenth century', in Davis and Ginsborg (eds), *Society and Politics in the Age of the Risorgimento*.

41 M. Barbagli, 'Marriage and the family in Italy in the early nineteenth century', ibid., p. 124.

42 Gibson, *Prostitution and the State in Liberal Italy*, p. 20.

43 M. L. Berti, 'La questione sanitaria a Cremona: problemi e provvedimenti,

1830–1880', *Storia Urbana*, 3, 1977, 71–89.

44   A. Forti Messina, 'Il colera e le condizione igenico sanitare di Napoli nel 1836–37', *Storia Urbana*, 3, 1977, p. 4, P. Preto, *Epidemia, paura e politica nell'Italia moderna* (Bari, 1987), p. 138.

45   Basing his evidence on Northern Europe, Richard Evans argues that it was police controls, rather than cholera epidemics themselves, that produced rioting: 'Epidemics and revolutions: cholera in nineteenth century Europe', *Past and Present*, 120, 1988, pp. 123–46.

46   Barbagli, 'Marriage and the family', pp. 122–7.

47   L. Guidi and L. Valenti, 'Malattia, povertà, devianza femminile, follia nelle istitutzioni napoletane di pubblica beneficenza', in Massafra (ed.), *Il mezzogiorno preunitario*, p. 1179.

48   S. J. Woolf, 'The poor and how to relieve them: the Restoration debate on poverty in Italy and Europe', in Davis and Ginsborg (eds), *Society and Politics in the Age of the Risorgimento*, pp. 62–9, and 'Segregazione sociale e attività politica nelle città italiane', pp. 26–7.

49   Davis, *Conflict and Control*, pp. 69–71, 105–11.

50   ibid., p. 76.

4   THE RISORGIMENTO AND ECONOMIC DEVELOPMENT

1   L. Cafagna, 'Introduzione', in *Dualismo e sviluppo nella storia d'Italia* (Venice, 1989), p. xii.

2   E. Sereni, *Capitalismo e mercato nazionale* (Rome, 1966). See also his earlier work, more specifically concerned with agrarian structures, *Il Capitalismo nelle campagne (1860–1900)* (Turin, 1947).

3   R. Romeo, *Risorgimento e capitalismo* (Bari, 1959).

4   A. Gerschenkron, 'Rosario Romeo and the original accumulation of capital', in *Economic Backwardness in Historical Perspective* (Cambridge, Mass., 1966).

5   G. Federico, 'Di un nuovo modello dell'industria italiana', *Società e Storia*, 8, 1980, p. 447.

6   S. Pollard, *Peaceful Conquest. The Industrialisation of Europe, 1760–1970* (Oxford, 1981), p. vii.

7   K. R. Greenfield, *Economics and Liberalism in the Risorgimento. A Study of Nationalism in Lombardy, 1814–1848* (Baltimore, 1934), pp. 4–9.

8   A. Dewerpe, *L'Industrie aux champs. Essai sur la proto-industrialisation en Italie du nord* (Rome, 1985).

9   A. Cento Bull, 'Proto-industrialisation, small-scale capital accumulation and diffused entrepreneurship: the case of the Brianza in Lombardy (1860–1950)', *Social History*, 14, 1989, p. 179.

10   G. Mori, ' Industrie senza industrializzazione: la peninsola italiana dalla fine della dominazione francese all'unità nazionale (1815–1861)', *Studi Storici*, 30, 1989, pp. 603–35.

11   F. Ramella, *Terra e telai. Sistema di parentela e manifattura nel biellese dell'ottocento* (Turin, 1983), A. Cento Bull, 'The Lombard silk industry in the 19th century: an industrial workforce in a rural setting' *The Italianist*, 7, 1987, pp. 99–121, and 'Proto-industrialisation and the Brianza in Lombardy'.

12 L. Cafagna, 'La prima onda industriale' and 'I modelli interpretativi della storiografia', both in *Dualismo e sviluppo*, F. Bonelli, 'Il capitalismo italiano: linee generali di interpretazione', in *Storia d'Italia, Annali*, vol. I (Turin, 1978).

13 Cafagna, 'Introduzione', in *Dualismo e sviluppo*, pp. xxix–xlii.

14 J. Davis, 'Remapping Italy's path to the twentieth century', *Journal of Modern History*, forthcoming, 1994.

15 Cafagna, 'I modelli interpretativi della storiografia', in *Dualismo e sviluppo*, p. 399.

16 Mori, 'Industrie senza industrializzazione', p. 606.

17 L. de Rosa, *Iniziativa e capitale straniero nell'industria metalmeccanica del mezzogiorno 1840–1904* (Naples, 1968).

18 E. Iachello and A. Signorelli, 'Borghesie urbane dell'ottocento', in M. Aymard and G. Giarrizzo (eds), *Storia d'Italia. Le regioni dall'unità a oggi. La Sicilia* (Turin, 1987), R. Battaglia, *Mercanti e imprenditori in una città marittima. Il caso di Messina (1850–1900)* (Milan, 1992), F. Benigno, 'Fra mare e terra: orizzonte economico e mutamento sociale in una città meridionale. Trapani nella prima metà dell'ottocento', in A. Massafra (ed.), *Il mezzogiorno preunitario. Economia, società, istituzioni* (Bari, 1988).

19 R. Battaglia, 'Qualità e trasformazione del ceto mercantile siciliano a metà dell'ottocento', in Massafra (ed.), *Il mezzogiorno preunitario*.

20 M. Salvadori, *Il mito del buongoverno. La questione meridionale da Cavour a Gramsci* (Turin, 1960).

21 P. Bevilacqua, 'Agricoltura e storia delle campagne nel mezzogiorno d'Italia', *Studi Storici*, 23, 1982, p. 676, 'Uomini, terre, economie', in P. Bevilacqua and A. Placanica (eds), *Storia d'Italia. Le regioni dall'unità a oggi. La Calabria* (Turin, 1985).

22 F. Assante, 'Le trasformazioni del paesaggio agrario', in Massafra (ed.), *Il mezzogiorno preunitario*, p. 22.

23 M. Petrusewicz, *Latifondo. Economia morale e vita materiale in una periferia dell'ottocento* (Venice, 1989), pp. xxiii–xxiv.

24 Letter to the *Times Literary Supplement (TLS)*, 4623, 8 November 1991, p. 15. De Vivo is commenting on Adrian Lyttleton's review article 'A new past for the Mezzogiorno', *TLS*, 4618, 4 October 4 1991, pp. 14–15, which discusses revisionist interpretations of the South. For John Davis's reply, defending Petrusewicz, see *TLS*, 4626, 29 November 1991, p. 19; for Piero Bevilacqua's reply see *TLS*, 4627, 6 December 1991, p. 15; and for de Vivo's reply to Davis and Bevilacqua see *TLS*, 4630, 27 December 1991, p. 13.

25 V. Giura, 'Infrastrutture, manifatture, commercio', in Massafra (ed.), *Il mezzogiorno preunitario*, p. 241.

26 P. Bevilacqua, *Breve storia dell'Italia meridionale dall'ottocento a oggi* (Rome, 1993), pp. 16–17.

27 A. Placanica, 'I caratteri originali', and P. Bevilacqua, 'Uomini, terre, economie', in Bevilacqua and Placanica (eds), *La Calabria*.

28 J. A. Davis, 'Technology and innovation in an industrial late-comer: Italy in the nineteenth century', in P. Matthias and J. A. Davis (eds), *Innovation and Technology in Europe. From the Eighteenth Century to the Present Day* (Oxford, 1991).

29 Mori, 'Industrie senza industrializzazione', p. 607.

90   *Notes*

30 L. Cafagna, 'La questione delle origini del dualismo economico italiano', in *Dualismo e sviluppo*, pp. 187, 217.
31 Mori, 'Industrie senza industrializzazione', pp. 607–8.

5 THE RISORGIMENTO AND ITALIAN NATIONALISM

1 B. Tobia, *Una patria per gli italiani. Spazi, itinerari, monumenti nell'Italia unita (1870–1900)* (Bari–Rome, 1991), S. Lanaro, *L'Italia nuova. Identità e sviluppo (1861–1988)* (Turin, 1988).
2 For example: M. Castelli, *Il conte di Cavour. Ricordi* (Turin, 1886), G. Massari, *Uomini di destra* (Turin, 1888), M. Minghetti, *I miei ricordi* (Turin, 1888–90), G. Pallavicino, *Memorie* (Turin, 1882–95), J. White Mario, *Vita di Garibaldi* (Milan, 3rd edn, 1882) and *Agostino Bertani e i suoi tempi* (Florence, 1888).
3 G. H. von Treitschke, *Historische und politische Aufsätze, vornehmlich zur neuesten deutschen Geschichte* (Leipzig, 1865), M. Paléologue, *Cavour, un grand réaliste* (Paris, 1926; Eng. trans. London, 1927).
4 D. Mack Smith, *Cavour and Garibaldi, 1860. A Study in Political Conflict* (Cambridge, 2nd edn, 1985).
5 A. Blumberg, *A Carefully Planned Accident. The Italian War of 1859* (London, 1990).
6 A. Galante Garrone, *I radicali in Italia (1849–1925)* (Milan, 1973), p. 23.
7 C. Lovett, *The Democratic Movement in Italy, 1830–1876* (Cambridge, Mass., 1982), p. 165.
8 J. Breuilly, *Nationalism and the State* (London, 2nd edn, 1985), p. 65.
9 R. Grew, 'Catholicism and the Risorgimento', in F. Coppa (ed.), *Studies in Modern Italian History. From the Risorgimento to the Republic* (New York, 1986), p. 47.
10 Quoted in G. Candeloro, *Storia dell'Italia moderna*, vol. II, *Dalla restaurazione alla rivoluzione nazionale* (Milan, 1958), pp. 211–13.
11 F. della Peruta, 'Mazzini della letteratura militante all'impegno politico', *Studi Storici*, 14, 1973, pp. 449–556.
12 P. Ginsborg, 'Risorgimento rivoluzionario. Mito e realtà di una guerra di popolo', *Storia e Dossier*, 47, 1991, pp. 61–97.
13 ibid., pp. 85–90.
14 P. Ginsborg, *Daniele Manin and the Venetian Revolution of 1848–49* (Cambridge, 1979), p. 377.
15 E. di Ciommo, *La nazione possibile. Mezzogiorno e questione nazionale nel 1848* (Milan, 1993), p. 51.
16 F. della Peruta, 'Il Risorgimento fra mito e realtà', *Risorgimento. Mito e realtà* (Milan, 1992), p. 11.
17 R. J. M. Olson, 'In the Dawn of Italy', *Ottocento. Romanticism and Revolution in 19th Century Italian Painting* (New York, 1992), pp. 13–25.
18 A. Lyttleton, 'The national question in Italy', in M. Teich and R. Porter (eds), *The National Question in Europe in Historical Context* (Cambridge, 1993), pp. 72–5.
19 M. Berengo, 'Intellettuali e organizzazione della cultura nell'età della Restaurazione', in E. Raponi (ed.), *Dagli stati preunitari d'antico regime all'unificazione* (Bologna, 1981), pp. 329–33.

20 Lyttleton, 'The national question in Italy', p. 89.
21 U. Carpi, *Letteratura e società nella Toscana del risorgimento. Gli intellettuali dell'Antologia* (Bari, 1974), A. Galante Garrone and F. della Peruta, *La stampa italiana del risorgimento* (Rome–Bari, 1979), A. Gernert, *Liberalismus als Handlungskonzept. Studien zur Rolle der politischen Presse im italienischen Risorgimento vor 1848* (Stuttgart, 1990).
22 S. Patriarca, 'Numbers and the Nation. The Statistical Representation of Italy, 1820–1871' (Johns Hopkins University, Ph.D. thesis, 1992), pp. 6, 97.
23 R. Grew, *A Sterner Plan for Italian Unity. The National Society in the Risorgimento* (Princeton, 1963), pp. 261–76.
24 ibid., pp. 111–23, 298–304, 312–41.
25 Lyttleton, 'The national question in Italy', p. 84.
26 F. Rizzi, *La coccarda e le campane. Comunità rurali e repubblica romana nel Lazio (1848–1849)* (Milan, 1989), A. de Clementi, *Vivere nel latifondo. Le comunità della Campagna laziale fra '700 e '800* (Milan, 1989).
27 Grew, 'Catholicism and the Risorgimento', p. 48.
28 ibid., p. 48.

6 NATIONAL UNIFICATION AND THE 'POST-RISORGIMENTO'

1 C.F. Delzell (ed.), *The Unification of Italy, 1859–61. Cavour, Mazzini or Garibaldi?* (New York, 1965), p. 1.
2 F. Chabod, *Storia della politica estera italiana dal 1870 al 1896*. vol. I, *Le premesse* (Bari, 1951).
3 K. Wegert, 'Contention with civility: the state and social control in the German Southwest, 1760–1850', *Historical Journal*, 34, 1991, p. 361.
4 L. Riall, 'Elite resistance to state formation: the case of Italy', in M. Fulbrook (ed.), *National Histories and European History* (London, 1993), pp. 59–63.
5 J. Breuilly, 'Conclusion: national peculiarities?', in *Labour and Liberalism in Nineteenth Century Europe* (Manchester, 1992), pp. 276–9.
6 S. Soldani, 'Risorgimento', in F. Levi, U. Levra, N. Tranfaglia (eds), *Storia d'Italia*, vol. III (Florence, 1978), p. 1132.
7 R. Grew, 'Catholicism and the Risorgimento', in F. Coppa (ed.), *Studies in Modern Italian History. From the Risorgimento to the Republic* (New York, 1986), p. 50.

Bibliography

Helpful introductions to historiographical issues can be found in D. Beales, *The Risorgimento and the Unification of Italy* (London, 2nd edn, 1981), ch. 1, and H. Hearder, *Italy in the Age of the Risorgimento, 1790–1870* (London, 1983), ch. 1. Those wishing to investigate further should consult S. J. Woolf (ed.), *The Italian Risorgimento* (London, 1969), especially the introduction and part II, and C. F. Delzell (ed.), *The Unification of Italy, 1859–61. Cavour, Mazzini or Garibaldi?* (New York, 1965). Readers can get a sense of the historical controversies over the Risorgimento and Italian unification by comparing Benedetto Croce's *A History of Italy, 1871–1915*, trans. C. M. Ady (Oxford, 1929) with Antonio Gramsci's 'Notes on Italian history', in *Selections from the Prison Notebooks of Antonio Gramsci* ed. and trans. Q. Hoare and G. Nowell Smith, (London, 1971). For an interesting and accessible analysis of Croce as a historian and politician, see D. Mack Smith, 'Benedetto Croce', *Journal of Contemporary History*, 8, 1973, pp. 41–61. The main ideas behind the post-war Anglo-American approach to the Risorgimento are well presented in the author's introduction to the second edition of D. Mack Smith, *Cavour and Garibaldi, 1860. A Study in Political Conflict* (Cambridge, 2nd edn, 1985), H. Stuart Hughes, 'The aftermath of the Risorgimento in four successive interpretations', *American Historical Review*, LXI/1, 1955, pp. 70–6, and A.W. Salamone (ed.), *Italy from Liberalism to Fascism. An Inquiry into the Origins of the Totalitarian State* (New York, 1970).

For a more up-to-date discussion, dealing specifically with the 'revisionist' approach but focusing more on the period after unification, John Davis's 'Remapping Italy's path to the twentieth century', *Journal of Modern History*, 1994, is particularly helpful. It is also useful as a general introduction to debates about Restoration government, Italian society and economic development. Some discussion of the revisionist agenda, but again focusing on the period after unification, is provided by Raffaele Romanelli, 'Political debate, social history and the Italian *borghesia*: changing perspectives in historical research', *Journal of Modern History*, 63/4, 1991, 717–39. The 'afterword' to Franco Rizzi's *La coccarda e le campane. Comunità rurali e repubblica romana nel Lazio (1848–1849)* (Milan, 1989) and the introduction to Paolo Macry's *Ottocento. Famiglia, élites e patrimoni a Napoli* (Turin, 1988) are interesting as position statements from revisionist historians. Piero Bevilacqua's introduction to his *Breve storia dell'Italia meridionale dall'ottocento a oggi* (Rome, 1993) is a concise statement of the revisionist approach to the South from a leading economic historian; A. Lyttleton, 'A new past for the Mezzogiorno', *Times Literary Supplement*, 4618, 4 October 1991, pp. 14–15, is the most accessible summary in English.

S. J. Woolf, *A History of Italy, 1700–1860. The Social Constraints of Political Change* (London, 1979), Beales, *The Risorgimento and the Unification of Italy*, Hearder, *Italy in the Age of the Risorgimento*, and F. J. Coppa, *The Origins of the Italian Wars of Independence* (London, 1992), are good narrative accounts of the Risorgimento. Woolf's study is the most detailed and concentrates more on social and economic change; Coppa's focuses on the diplomatic and military aspects of unification. J. A. Davis, *Conflict and Control. Law and Order in Nineteenth Century Italy* (London, 1988), is not only a valuable introduction to the subject of law and order but is useful as a broad guide to the new social history in Italy. In Italian, Giorgio Candeloro's multi-volume *Storia dell' Italia moderna* (Milan, 1956–78), written from a Marxist perspective, is very helpful (Volumes 1 to 5 cover the Risorgimento and national unification), while A. Scirocco, *L'Italia del risorgimento* (Bologna, 1990) is clear, concise and very up to date. The contributions to Angelo Massafra's wide-ranging *Il mezzogiorno preunitario. Economia, società, istituzioni* (Bari, 1988) are an invaluable introduction to the history of Southern Italy before unification.

Hearder, *Italy in the Age of the Risorgimento*, has a lot of detail on Restoration government but his analysis overemphasises the reactionary elements. Frank Coppa's study of *Cardinal Giacomo Antonelli and Papal Politics in European Affairs* (Albany, 1990) offers some fascinating insights into the career of Pius IX's secretary of state, and indicates that Antonelli's reputation as a reactionary needs to be modified. A. J. Reinerman, *Austria and the Papacy in the Age of Metternich*, 2 vols (Washington, DC, 1979–89), contains good discussions of Metternich's Italian policy and the policy of 'amalgamation'. A significant part of O. Chadwick, *The Popes and European Revolution* (Oxford, 1981), is concerned with Italy; Chapter 8 deals with the Restoration period.

Unfortunately, since so little historical research in Italy has been translated into English, a knowledge of Italian is essential if specific subjects are to be studied in any detail. The revisionist approach to Restoration government is represented in studies of pre-unification Italy published by UTET of Turin: M. Caravale and A. Caracciolo, *Lo Stato Pontificio da Martino V a Pio X* (Turin, 1978), M. Meriggi, *Il regno Lombardo-Veneto* (Turin, 1987), and V. d'Alessandro and G. Giarrizzo, *La Sicilia dal vespro al' unità d'Italia* (Turin, 1989), have appeared so far. Also very useful on the policies of the reactionary Prince of Canosa and of conservative reformer de Medici in Naples is G. Cingari, *Mezzogiorno e risorgimento. La restaurazione a Napoli dal 1821 al 1830* (Bari, 1970). On the reforms of Carlo Alberto in Piedmont, the most important study to have appeared in recent years is N. Nada, *Dallo stato assoluto allo stato costituzionale. Storia del regno di Carlo Alberto dal 1831 al 1848* (Turin, 1980), which seeks to 'rescue' Carlo Alberto from the negative judgements of nationalist historiography. For an approach to Lombardy-Venetia which redefines the relationship between the Lombard elites and the Austrian administration, see M. Meriggi, *Amministrazione e classi sociali nel Lombardo-Veneto 1814–1848* (Bologna, 1983), and, for an important study of Venetia in the early

Restoration period, see D. Lavan, 'Studies in the Habsburg Administration of Venetia, 1814–1835' (Cambridge University, Ph.D. thesis, 1991). Meriggi provides a wealth of information about the effect of administrative centralisation on relations between classes, and between state and society. A broadly similar approach is adopted in A. Scirocco, 'L'amministrazione civile: istituzioni, funzionari, carriere', and A. Spagnoletti, 'Centri e periferie nello stato napoletano del primo ottocento', both in Massafra (ed.), *Il mezzogiorno preunitario*. P. Pezzino, 'Monarchia amministrativa ed *élites* locali: Naro nella prima metà dell'ottocento,' in P. Pezzino, *Un paradiso abitato dai diavoli. Società, élites, istituzioni nel mezzogiorno contemporaneo* (Milan, 1992), and F. Rizzi, 'Pourquoi obéir a l'état? Une communauté rurale du Latium aux XVIIIᵉ et XIXᵉ siècles', *Etudes Rurales*, 101–2, 1986, pp. 271–87, look at the conflicts between central and local power in individual communes. Those wishing to know more about the relations between popular classes and the Restoration governments should start with A. J. Reinerman, 'The failure of popular counter-revolution in Risorgimento Italy: the case of the centurions, 1831–1847', *The Historical Journal*, 34, 1991, pp. 21–41.

There are no general surveys of Italian society in this period: as an introduction, Woolf, *A History of Italy*, and Davis, *Conflict and Control*, should be consulted. Although many of the findings in K. R. Greenfield, *Economics and Liberalism in the Risorgimento. A study of Nationalism in Lombady, 1814–1848* (Baltimore, 1934) have been challenged, it is still useful as a general account of social and economic change in Lombardy. Davis's 'Introduction: Antonio Gramsci and Italy's passive revolution' and P. Ginsborg, 'Gramsci and the era of bourgeois revolution in Italy', both in J. A. Davis (ed.), *Gramsci and Italy's Passive Revolution* (London, 1979), are critical analyses of the Risorgimento as 'passive revolution'. For a history of the Risorgimento as a failed bourgeois revolution, see L. Cafagna, 'Se il risorgimento italiano sia stato una "rivoluzione borghese"', in *Dualismo e sviluppo nella storia d'Italia* (Venice, 1989). There is a substantial and growing literature on elites and middle classes in nineteenth-century Italy; of this literature, probably the most innovative works are Macry, *Ottocento* (on aristocratic families in Naples), and A. M. Banti, *Terra e denaro. Una borghesia padana dell'ottocento* (Venice, 1989) (on the agrarian bourgeoisie of Piacenza). These studies are more concerned with the later nineteenth century, as is A. Lyttleton, 'The middle classes in Liberal Italy', in J. A. Davis and P. Ginsborg (eds), *Society and Politics in the Age of the Risorgimento* (Cambridge, 1991). M. Meriggi, 'La borghesia italiana', in J. Kocka (ed.), *Borghesie europee dell'ottocento* (Venice, 1989) includes a discussion of the Italian bourgeoisie prior to unification. There are a number of local studies of the new associational life of urban elites in A. M. Banti and M. Meriggi (eds), 'Élites e associazioni nell'Italia dell'ottocento', *Quaderni Storici*, 77/2, 1991, and M. Meriggi, *Milano borghese. Circoli ed elites nell'ottocento* (Venice, 1993), and local studies of Southern elites in Massafra (ed.), *Il mezzogiorno preunitario*.

A. de Clementi, *Vivere nel latifondo. Le comunità della campagna laziale fra '700 e '800* (Milan, 1989), and M. Caffiero, 'Usi e abusi: comunità rurali e difesa dell'economia tradizionale nello stato pontificio', *Passato e Presente*, 24, 1990, pp. 73–93, both look at the impact of social and economic change in local communities in Lazio. On the condition of the peasantry and protest against changes in land-use patterns, see P. Brunello, *Ribelli, questuanti e banditi*.

Proteste contadine in Veneto e in Friuli, 1814–1866 (Venice, 1981). Paul Ginsborg looks at the forms and repression of banditry in Venetia in 'After the revolution: bandits on the plains of the Po 1848–54'; Giovanna Fiume analyses the relations between bandits and local power in Sicily in 'Bandits, violence and the organisation of power in Sicily in the early nineteenth century'; both are in Davis and Ginsborg (eds), *Society and Politics in the Age of the Risorgimento*. For an innovative analysis of the relationship between bandits and the state see M. Petrusewicz, 'Society against the state: peasant brigandage in Southern Italy', *Criminal Justice History* 8, 1987, pp. 1–20. Those interested in the variety of approaches to criminality in Southern Italy should also look at the contributions in Massafra (ed.), *Il mezzogiorno preunitario*.

E. Sori (ed.), *Città e controllo sociale in Italia tra XVIII e XIX secolo* (Milan, 1982), is perhaps the best place to start reading about the conditions of the urban poor. More general information about conditions in the capital cities of Restoration Italy is in *Le città capitale degli stati pre-unitari. Atti del LIII Congresso del Istituto per la Storia del Risorgimento Italiano. 1986* (Rome, 1988). P. Preto, *Epidemia, paura e politica nell'Italia moderna* (Bari, 1987), has a good general discussion of the effect of epidemics in urban centres. U. Levra, *L'altro volto del Torino risorgimentale. 1814–1848* (Turin, 1989), studies the conditions of the urban poor, relations between classes and forms of social control in Turin. On responses to poverty and charitable institutions, see S. J. Woolf, 'The poor and how to relieve them: the Restoration debate on poverty in Italy and Europe', and M. Barbagli, 'Marriage and the family in Italy in the early nineteenth century'; both are in Davis and Ginsborg (eds), *Society and Politics in the Age of the Risorgimento*. The same volume also contains an invaluable general survey of women and work by Simonetta Ortaggi Cammarosano, 'Labouring women in Northern and Central Italy in the nineteenth century'. Mary Gibson, *Prostitution and the State in Liberal Italy* (New Brunswick, 1986), is an excellent general study of prostitution and has some useful information on the Risorgimento period.

On economic development, the best starting-point is L. Cafagna, 'The industrial revolution in Italy, 1830–1914', in C. Cipolla (ed.), *The Fontana Economic History of Europe*, vol. IV (London, 1973). Readers with a knowledge of Italian may also wish to consult the collection of his essays on Italian economic development, *Dualismo e sviluppo nella storia d'Italia*. G. Toniolo, *An Economic History of Liberal Italy 1850–1918* (London, 1990), is a recent overview but has little on the Risorgimento as such. Unfortunately, neither E. Sereni, *Il capitalismo nelle campagne (1860–1900)* (Turin, 1947), nor R. Romeo, *Risorgimento e capitalismo* (Bari, 1959), has been published in English, so only readers of Italian will be able to get a sense of the ferocity of the debate between Marxists and liberals at this time (although both Woolf (ed.), *The Italian Risorgimento*, and Delzell (ed.), *The Unification of Italy*, have extracts from Romeo's book). A. Gerschenkron, 'Rosario Romeo and the original accumulation of capital', in *Economic Backwardness in Historical Perspective* (Cambridge, Mass., 1966), is a further contribution to this debate. Much of Cafagna's work represents an attempt to get away from this debate, as does F. Bonelli's 'Il capitalismo italiano: linee generali di interpretazione', in *Storia d'Italia, Annali*, vol. I (Turin, 1978). On Bonelli's work, see G. Federico, 'Di un nuovo modello dell'industria italiana', *Società e Storia*, 8, 1980, pp. 433–55.

On proto-industrialisation in Italy, see G. Mori, 'Il tempo della protoindustrializzazione' in G. Mori (ed.), *L'industrializzazione in Italia* (Bologna, 2nd edn, 1981), and the same author's 'Industrie senza industrializzazione: la peninsola italiana dalla fine della dominazione francese all'unità nazionale (1815–1861', *Studi Storici*, 30, 1989, pp. 603–35. Anna Bull has written two interesting and critical contributions to the proto-industrialisation debate, 'The Lombard silk spinners in the 19th century; an industrial workforce in a rural setting', *The Italianist*, 7, 1987, pp. 99–121, and 'Proto-industrialisation, small-scale capital accumulation and diffused entrepreneurship: the case of Brianza in Lombardy (1860–1950)', *Social History*, 14, 1989, pp. 177–200. The first two chapters of A. Bull and P. Corner, *From Peasant to Entrepreneur. The Survival of the Family Economy in Italy* (Oxford, 1993), are an extremely useful introduction to debates about the peasant economy in Italy during this period. F. Ramella, *Terra e telai. Sistema di parentela e manifattura nel biellese dell'ottocento* (Turin, 1983), uses the proto-industrial model for this 'micro' study of industry and kinship structures in Biella (Lombardy). On industry, agriculture and trade in the South, the best starting-point is again the contributions to Massafra (ed.), *Il mezzogiorno preunitario*. On the Southern *latifondo*, Denis Mack Smith has written a useful essay, 'The latifundia in modern Sicilian history', *Proceedings of the British Academy*, 51, 1965, pp. 85–124. For a classic statement of the backwardness of Southern agriculture, see M. Rossi Doria, 'The land tenure system and class in Southern Italy', *American Historical Review*, 64/1, 1958, pp. 46–53. As an antidote to the above analyses, M. Petrusewicz, *Latifondo. Economia morale e vita materiale in una periferia dell'ottocento* (Venice, 1989), and P. Bevilacqua, 'Uomini, terre, economie' in P. Bevilacqua and A. Placanica (eds), *Storia d'Italia. Le regioni dall'unità a oggi. La Calabria* (Turin, 1985), are stimulating and often convincing.

Although there is a vast literature on nationalist politics in the Risorgimento, little of it is very recent or takes account of revisionist debates. A. Lyttleton, 'The national question in Italy', in M. Teich and R. Porter (eds), *The National Question in Europe in Historical Context* (Cambridge, 1993), is the best survey to have appeared recently in English. There are also useful introductory analyses in the general surveys of the Risorgimento mentioned above. There is an interesting chapter in J. Breuilly, *Nationalism and the State* (Manchester, 2nd edn, 1985), that deals with the comparative unifications of Italy and Germany. R. Grew, 'Catholicism and the Risorgimento', in F. Coppa (ed.), *Studies in Modern Italian History. From the Risorgimento to the Republic* (New York, 1986), and P. Ginsborg, 'Risorgimento rivoluzionario: mito e realtà di una guerra di popolo', *Storia e Dossier*, 47, 1991, pp. 61–97, suggest the uses of an approach that focuses more on nationalist culture than on class.

On political struggle in the Risorgimento, Denis Mack Smith's, *Cavour* (London, 1985), written from a very critical perspective, is useful as an introductory biography but not nearly as rich as Rosario Romeo's more laudatory *Cavour e il suo tempo*, 3 vols (Bari, 1969–84). It is interesting to compare these works with M. Paléologue, *Cavour* (London, 1927), the classic account of Cavour as a political 'realist'. U. Carpi, 'Egemonia moderata e intellettuali nel risorgimento' in *Storia d'Italia, Annali, vol. IV, Intellettuali e potere* (Turin, 1981), is a good introduction to moderate liberal ideology, while M. d'Azeglio, *Things I Remember* (London, 1966), a personal memoir of the Risorgimento from one of its 'elder statesmen', is also useful. On Mazzini and

Mazzinian politics, F. della Peruta, *Mazzini e i rivoluzionari italiani* (Milan, 1974), *I democratici e la rivoluzione italiana* (Milan, 1958) and A. Scirocco, *I democratici italiani da Sapri a Porta Pia* (Naples, 1969), are probably the most important works. P. Ginsborg, *Daniele Manin and the Venetian Revolution of 1848–49* (Cambridge, 1979), is probably the best discussion in English of democratic politics; notwithstanding its regional focus, it is also very useful for its general consideration of the democratic movement in Italy. C. Lovett, *The Democratic Movement in Italy, 1830–1876* (Cambridge, Mass., 1982), analyses the experiences of democratic activists, also focusing on the reasons for their 'failure'. R. Grew, *A Sterner Plan for Italian Unity. The Italian National Society in the Risorgimento* (Princeton, 1963), is a fascinating study of the National Society and of its nationalist successes. E. di Ciommo, *La nazione possibile. Mezzogiorno e questione nazionale nel 1848* (Milan, 1993), is one of the few studies of nationalist politics from a revisionist historian; she looks at the construction of an idea of nationhood through the 1848 revolution in Southern Italy. Silvana Patriarca, 'Numbers and the Nation. The Statistical Representation of Italy, 1820–1871' (Johns Hopkins University, Ph.D. thesis, 1992), is a stimulating discussion of the role played by statistical analysis in the formation of nationalist ideas in Italy.

On Garibaldi, D. Mack Smith, *Garibaldi* (London, 1957), is a useful introduction, while F. della Peruta, 'Garibaldi tra mito e politico', in *Conservatori, liberali e democratici nel risorgimento* (Milan, 1989), is interesting but never really analyses the reason for Garibaldi's appeal; neither do the various contributions to *Giuseppe Garibaldi e il suo mito. Atti del LI Congresso di Storia del Risorgimento Italiano* (Rome, 1984). R. Battaglia (ed.), *Garibaldi e il socialismo* (Rome, 1984), is an important analysis of Garibaldi's involvement with socialist movements. On the events of 1860, the classic account is D. Mack Smith, *Cavour and Garibaldi. A Study in Political Conflict* (Cambridge, 2nd edn, 1985), while the same author has written an important analysis of peasant rebellion in Sicily, 'The peasants' revolt in Sicily, 1860', in *Victor Emmanuel, Cavour and the Risorgimento* (Oxford, 1971). G. C. Abba, *The Diary of One of Garibaldi's Thousand* (Oxford, 1962), is a fascinating and very readable memoir of a volunteer in Garibaldi's expedition to Sicily.

Mack Smith has written a controversial history of Italy after unification, *Italy: A Modern History* (Ann Arbor, 1959), which stresses the disappointments of the 'post-Risorgimento'. C. Seton Watson, *Italy from Liberalism to Fascism* (London, 1968), is an excellent and very wide-ranging introduction to Liberal Italy. M. Clark, *Modern Italy, 1871–1982* (London, 1985), is also useful. In Italian, R. Romanelli, *L'Italia liberale* (Bologna, 1979), is a good, and fairly up-to-date, general survey. For an analysis of recent literature, which focuses on the relations between central and local power, see L. Riall, 'Elite resistance to state formation: the case of Italy', in M. Fulbrook (ed.), *National Histories and European History* (London, 1993).

Index